Maximizing Profits with WooCommerce: The Ultimate Guide to Dropshipping from AliExpress

---

Table of Contents

Introduction
1. Understanding Dropshipping: The Basics
2. Why Choose WooCommerce and AliExpress?

Chapter 1: Setting Up Your Online Store
1.1. Choosing the Right Domain and Hosting
1.2. Installing and Setting Up WooCommerce
1.3. Essential WooCommerce Settings for Dropshipping
1.4. Designing a User-Friendly Website

Chapter 2: Integrating AliExpress with WooCommerce
2.1. Selecting Products to Sell
2.2. Using AliExpress Dropshipping Plugins
2.3. Automating Product Import from AliExpress
2.4. Managing AliExpress Orders Efficiently

Chapter 3: Enhancing Your Store with Essential Plugins
3.1. SEO Optimization Tools
3.2. Payment Gateway Integrations
3.3. Advanced Analytics Plugins
3.4. Email Marketing and Automation Tools

Chapter 4: Mastering Dropshipping Operations
4.1. Inventory Management Strategies
4.2. Handling Shipping and Delivery
4.3. Dealing with Returns and Refunds
4.4. Providing Excellent Customer Service

Chapter 5: Marketing Your Dropshipping Store
5.1. Developing a Strong Brand Identity
5.2. Effective Social Media Strategies
5.3. Leveraging Email Marketing
5.4. Using Paid Advertising Effectively

Chapter 6: Scaling Your Dropshipping Business
6.1. Expanding Your Product Range
6.2. Optimizing for Higher Conversion Rates
6.3. Collaborating with Influencers and Affiliates
6.4. Exploring International Markets

Chapter 7: Legal and Financial Considerations
7.1. Understanding Dropshipping Legalities
7.2. Tax Implications and Compliance

7.3. Setting Up Business Finances
7.4. Protecting Your Business with Insurances

Chapter 8: Advanced Dropshipping Strategies
8.1. Utilizing Data for Business Decisions
8.2. Exploring Multi-channel Selling
8.3. Customization and Private Labeling
8.4. Building a Sustainable Business Model

Conclusion
- Summary of Key Takeaways
- Future Trends in Dropshipping

Appendices
- List of Recommended WooCommerce and AliExpress Plugins
- Additional Resources for Learning and Support

This outline provides a comprehensive guide for individuals looking to make money through a WooCommerce-based dropshipping business using AliExpress. Each chapter is designed to cover all the essential aspects of setting up, running, and scaling a successful online store, with a focus on practical tips, tools, and strategies.

Understanding Dropshipping: The Basics

In today's fast-paced e-commerce landscape, entrepreneurs and online business owners are constantly on the lookout for innovative ways to maximize profits and expand their reach. One such strategy that has gained immense popularity in recent years is dropshipping. If you're an aspiring online retailer or an established business owner looking to streamline operations and enhance your profit margins, then you're in the right place.

Welcome to "Maximizing Profits with WooCommerce: The Ultimate Guide to Dropshipping from AliExpress." In this comprehensive guide, we will take you on a journey through the world of dropshipping, a business model that has revolutionized the way products are sourced, sold, and shipped. More specifically, we will delve into the intricacies of using WooCommerce, one of the leading e-commerce platforms, in conjunction with AliExpress, the global online marketplace, to create a highly profitable dropshipping venture.

Before we dive into the nitty-gritty details of setting up your WooCommerce store and establishing a successful AliExpress dropshipping operation, let's start with the fundamentals. What exactly is dropshipping, and why has it become the go-to method for countless online entrepreneurs? What are the key benefits and challenges associated with this business model? How can you leverage the power of WooCommerce and AliExpress to unlock your full potential as a dropshipper?

In this opening section, we will answer these critical questions and lay the foundation for your journey into the world of dropshipping. By understanding the basics, you'll gain the knowledge and confidence needed to embark on a profitable e-commerce adventure that can transform your business and financial future.

So, whether you're a seasoned online retailer or someone exploring e-commerce for the first time, let's embark on this exciting journey together. Get ready to uncover the strategies, tools, and insights that will empower you to maximize your profits with WooCommerce and AliExpress dropshipping. Let's begin by unraveling the essence of dropshipping and why it's a game-changer in the world of online business.

Why Choose WooCommerce and AliExpress?

In the dynamic landscape of e-commerce, success often hinges on making strategic choices. Every decision you make as an online business owner has the potential to impact your profitability, scalability, and customer satisfaction. In this journey to maximize profits and streamline operations, one of the most powerful combinations at your disposal is the fusion of WooCommerce and AliExpress.

Welcome to "Maximizing Profits with WooCommerce: The Ultimate Guide to Dropshipping from AliExpress." In the pages that follow, we will embark on an expedition into the world of dropshipping, unveiling the transformative capabilities that lie within this dynamic partnership. Together, we'll explore the reasons why WooCommerce, a versatile and user-friendly e-commerce platform, harmonizes seamlessly with AliExpress, the global marketplace giant.

But first, let's address the fundamental question: Why should you choose WooCommerce and AliExpress as the pillars of your dropshipping venture?

WooCommerce, as a feature-rich and customizable e-commerce solution, empowers you to create a unique and branded online store tailored to your specific needs. With its extensive array of plugins and themes, WooCommerce provides the flexibility to design a store that aligns with your vision, while also offering a user-friendly interface that ensures an exceptional shopping experience for your customers. Whether you're a seasoned e-commerce veteran or a newcomer to online retail, WooCommerce offers the tools and support you need to succeed.

Now, pair WooCommerce with AliExpress, and you unlock a world of possibilities. AliExpress, known for its vast product catalog and global network of suppliers, serves as a treasure trove for dropshippers. With millions of products spanning various categories, AliExpress provides an unparalleled range of choices, allowing you to curate a product lineup that resonates with your target audience. Moreover, its competitive pricing and efficient shipping options enable you to stay ahead in a fiercely competitive market.

In this guide, we will delve deep into the synergy between WooCommerce and AliExpress, showcasing how this partnership can be a game-changer for your dropshipping business. You'll learn how to seamlessly integrate AliExpress suppliers into your WooCommerce store, automate order fulfillment, manage inventory, and optimize your product listings for maximum conversions.

So, whether you're just starting your journey as an online entrepreneur or seeking to elevate your existing e-commerce venture, join us as we uncover the strategic advantages of choosing WooCommerce and AliExpress as your trusted allies in the pursuit of maximizing profits. Let's embark on this exciting journey together, harnessing the immense potential that lies within this dynamic duo.

Chapter 1: Setting Up Your Online Store

Welcome to the first chapter of "Maximizing Profits with WooCommerce: The Ultimate Guide to Dropshipping from AliExpress." In this chapter, we will embark on the crucial first steps of your dropshipping journey: setting up your online store. Building a strong foundation is essential for the success of your e-commerce venture, and it all begins here.

In the vast realm of online retail, your store serves as your digital storefront, your brand ambassador, and your customer's gateway to your products and services. It's where the magic happens, where potential buyers become loyal customers, and where your revenue stream flows. Therefore, it's paramount that you establish an online store that not only reflects your brand identity but also provides an exceptional shopping experience.

We understand that creating an online store might seem daunting, especially if you're new to e-commerce. However, with the power of WooCommerce, a versatile and user-friendly e-commerce platform, and the abundant resources available through AliExpress, you'll find that the process can be streamlined and straightforward. Whether you're a tech-savvy entrepreneur or a non-technical business owner, this guide will walk you through every step, making the setup process accessible to all.

By the end of this chapter, you will have a fully functional WooCommerce store ready to showcase your products and attract eager customers. We'll cover essential topics such as domain registration, hosting selection, WooCommerce installation, and store configuration. With these elements in place, you'll be well on your way to creating a robust online presence that sets the stage for your dropshipping success.

So, if you're ready to roll up your sleeves and take the first exciting steps towards building your online store, let's dive into the world of WooCommerce setup. It's time to transform your vision into a digital reality and create a captivating online shopping destination that will drive profits and capture the hearts of your customers. Let's get started.

1.1 Choosing the Right Domain and Hosting

In the vast landscape of e-commerce, the foundation of your online store begins with two critical decisions: choosing the right domain name and selecting the perfect hosting solution. These choices may seem straightforward, but they hold immense significance for the success and functionality of your online venture.

Your domain name is your digital address, the web equivalent of your brick-and-mortar store's location. It's how your customers will find and remember you in the vast sea of websites. Hosting, on the other hand, is like the infrastructure of your online store – the engine that keeps everything running smoothly. Together, they form the bedrock of your e-commerce operation.

In this section, we will guide you through the process of selecting a domain name that aligns with your brand and business identity. We'll also explore the world of web hosting, helping you understand the different options available and how to choose the right hosting solution to ensure your online store's performance, security, and scalability.

By the end of this section, you'll be equipped with the knowledge and tools needed to make informed decisions regarding your domain name and hosting, setting the stage for a robust and reliable online store. So, let's dive in and get started on this essential aspect of your dropshipping journey.

1.2 Installing and Setting Up WooCommerce

Now that you've secured your domain name and hosting, it's time to transform your website into a fully functional e-commerce store by installing and configuring WooCommerce. WooCommerce is a powerful plugin for WordPress that enables you to build and manage your online store with ease. In this section, we will walk you through the steps to get WooCommerce up and running smoothly.

1. Install WordPress

Before we can dive into setting up WooCommerce, you need to have WordPress installed on your hosting server. WordPress is the most popular content management system (CMS) and serves as the foundation for countless websites and online stores.

Steps to Install WordPress:

1. Log in to your hosting account's control panel (usually cPanel).
2. Navigate to the "Auto Installers" or "One-Click Installs" section.
3. Locate WordPress in the list of available software and click on it.
4. Follow the on-screen instructions to install WordPress, ensuring you select your domain as the installation location.

Once WordPress is successfully installed, you can proceed to the next step.

2. Install the WooCommerce Plugin

With WordPress in place, it's time to add the WooCommerce plugin to your website. This plugin will turn your standard WordPress site into a feature-rich e-commerce platform.

Steps to Install WooCommerce:

1. Log in to your WordPress dashboard by visiting your domain followed by "/wp-admin" (e.g., www.yourwebsite.com/wp-admin).
2. In the WordPress dashboard, navigate to "Plugins" in the left-hand menu and click on "Add New."
3. In the search bar, type "WooCommerce" and press "Enter."
4. Find the WooCommerce plugin in the search results and click the "Install Now" button.
5. After installation, click "Activate" to activate the plugin.

3. Configure WooCommerce Settings

Now that WooCommerce is active on your website, it's time to configure its settings to align with your business needs and preferences. This includes setting your store's location, currency, payment methods, and shipping options.

Steps to Configure WooCommerce Settings:

1. In your WordPress dashboard, go to "WooCommerce" in the left-hand menu and click on "Settings."
2. Navigate through the tabs (General, Products, Shipping, Payments, etc.) and configure each section

according to your requirements.
3. Pay close attention to the "Payments" tab to set up your preferred payment gateways (e.g., PayPal, Stripe) to accept payments from customers.

4. Add Products to Your Store

With WooCommerce configured, it's time to populate your online store with products. You can manually add products or import them from your chosen AliExpress suppliers, a topic we'll cover in detail in later chapters.

Steps to Add Products:

1. In your WordPress dashboard, go to "Products" and click "Add New."
2. Fill in the product details, including title, description, price, and images.
3. Click "Publish" to make the product live on your website.

Congratulations! You've now successfully installed and set up WooCommerce on your website. Your online store is taking shape, and you're ready to start adding products and customizing your site's appearance. In the upcoming chapters, we'll explore how to integrate AliExpress suppliers and optimize your product listings for maximum profitability.

1.3 Essential WooCommerce Settings for Dropshipping

Now that you have WooCommerce installed on your website, it's time to fine-tune your online store for the dropshipping business model. WooCommerce offers a variety of settings that you can optimize to ensure smooth operations, efficient order management, and a seamless shopping experience for your customers. In this section, we will focus on the essential WooCommerce settings that are particularly important for a dropshipping venture.

1. General Settings

a. Store Address: Ensure that your store address is correctly set to match your location. This is crucial for calculating shipping costs and taxes accurately.

b. Selling Locations: Specify the regions and countries where you want to sell your products. For a global dropshipping store, consider enabling international sales.

2. Currency and Payments

a. Currency: Set your store's default currency to match the currency of your target audience. This ensures that product prices are displayed in a familiar currency for your customers.

b. Payment Gateways: Configure your payment gateways to accept payments from customers. Popular options include PayPal, Stripe, and credit card payments. Ensure that your chosen payment methods are well-suited for international transactions.

3. Shipping Settings

a. Shipping Zones: Define shipping zones for different regions. For a dropshipping store, you may have multiple shipping zones to accommodate various suppliers and shipping methods.

b. Shipping Methods: Choose the shipping methods you'll offer to customers. Consider providing options for standard shipping, express shipping, and any special services your suppliers offer.

c. Shipping Classes: Assign shipping classes to products based on their size, weight, or other relevant factors. This helps calculate accurate shipping rates for different products.

4. Tax Settings

a. Tax Options: Determine whether you need to charge taxes on your products and configure tax settings accordingly. Dropshipping businesses often have complex tax considerations due to international sales, so consult with a tax professional if needed.

5. Product Settings

a. Reviews and Ratings: Decide whether you want to enable product reviews and ratings. Customer feedback can build trust and credibility for your store.

b. Inventory Management: If you plan to manage your inventory through WooCommerce (recommended for dropshipping), make sure to set up inventory tracking for your products.

6. Email Notifications

a. Order Notifications: Configure email notifications for new orders, order status updates, and customer inquiries. This ensures you stay informed and can provide excellent customer service.

7. Security and Privacy

a. SSL Certificate: Ensure your website has an SSL certificate for secure data transmission, which is crucial for customer trust and online security.

8. Additional Settings

Explore additional WooCommerce settings that may be relevant to your specific business needs. WooCommerce is highly customizable, allowing you to tailor your store to your preferences.

By fine-tuning these essential WooCommerce settings for dropshipping, you'll create a solid foundation for your online business. In the upcoming chapters, we'll delve into more advanced topics such as integrating AliExpress suppliers, automating order fulfillment, and optimizing product listings to maximize your profits and streamline your dropshipping operations.

1.4 Designing a User-Friendly Website

A well-designed website is more than just aesthetically pleasing; it's the cornerstone of a positive user experience. In the competitive world of e-commerce, where first impressions matter, the design of your online store plays a pivotal role in attracting and retaining customers. In this section, we'll explore the key principles of designing a user-friendly website for your dropshipping venture.

1. Choose a Responsive Theme

Selecting the right theme for your WooCommerce store is a crucial decision. Ensure that your chosen theme is responsive, meaning it adapts seamlessly to different screen sizes and devices. A responsive theme guarantees that your website looks and functions well on desktops, tablets, and smartphones, providing a consistent and user-friendly experience for all visitors.

2. Optimize Page Loading Speed

Page loading speed is a critical factor in retaining visitors and improving your search engine rankings. Slow-loading pages can lead to high bounce rates and lost sales. To optimize your website's loading speed:

- Compress images and use appropriate image formats.
- Minimize the use of external scripts and plugins.
- Leverage browser caching.
- Consider a Content Delivery Network (CDN) to distribute content efficiently.

3. Intuitive Navigation

A user-friendly website should have a clear and intuitive navigation structure. Your customers should easily find the products they're looking for without frustration. Key tips for improving navigation include:

- Implementing a straightforward menu structure.
- Using descriptive categories and subcategories.
- Incorporating a search bar for quick product searches.
- Providing filters and sorting options for product listings.

4. High-Quality Product Images

In e-commerce, visuals are paramount. High-quality product images can significantly impact your sales. Ensure that your product images are clear, well-lit, and showcase products from various angles. Consider offering zoom functionality to allow customers to examine products closely.

5. Compelling Product Descriptions

Engage your customers with compelling product descriptions. Each product should have a detailed description that includes features, benefits, specifications, and any other relevant information. Use persuasive language to highlight the value of your products and address potential customer questions.

6. Mobile-Friendly Design

With an increasing number of customers shopping on mobile devices, a mobile-friendly design is no longer optional – it's essential. Test your website's mobile responsiveness and ensure that all features and functionalities work seamlessly on smartphones.

7. Streamlined Checkout Process

A complicated or lengthy checkout process can lead to cart abandonment. Streamline the checkout process by minimizing the number of steps and requesting only essential information. Offer guest checkout options to simplify the buying process for first-time customers.

8. Trust-Building Elements

Building trust with your customers is crucial for a successful dropshipping business. Incorporate trust-building elements, such as customer reviews and testimonials, secure payment icons, and clear privacy and return policies.

9. Regular Testing and Optimization

Website design is an ongoing process. Regularly test different elements, gather user feedback, and make data-driven optimizations to improve your site's usability and performance continually.

By implementing these principles of user-friendly website design, you'll create a digital storefront that not only attracts visitors but also converts them into loyal customers. In the upcoming chapters, we'll explore strategies to integrate AliExpress suppliers seamlessly, automate order processes, and enhance your product listings to maximize your dropshipping profits.

Chapter 2: Integrating AliExpress with WooCommerce

Welcome to the heart of your dropshipping journey! In Chapter 1, we laid the foundation for your online store, setting up WooCommerce and designing a user-friendly website. Now, it's time to dive into the heart of your dropshipping operation: integrating AliExpress with WooCommerce.

AliExpress, the global online marketplace, is a treasure trove of products and suppliers from around the world. It's the key to unlocking an extensive range of products, competitive prices, and reliable shipping options for your dropshipping business. By seamlessly integrating AliExpress with your WooCommerce store, you'll gain access to a vast catalog of items to offer your customers without the need for physical inventory.

In this chapter, we'll guide you through the process of integrating AliExpress with WooCommerce step by step. Whether you're new to dropshipping or looking to optimize your existing operation, you'll discover how to:

1. Find Reliable AliExpress Suppliers: We'll show you how to identify trustworthy suppliers with a track record of delivering quality products and reliable shipping.

2. Import Products to Your Store: Learn how to import AliExpress products to your WooCommerce store, including product details, images, and pricing.

3. Set Pricing and Profit Margins: Understand how to price your products competitively while ensuring a healthy profit margin.

4. Automate Order Fulfillment: Discover tools and strategies to streamline the order fulfillment process, so you can focus on growing your business.

5. Manage Inventory and Stock Levels: Keep track of your product inventory and availability to

prevent overselling and manage customer expectations.

6. Handle Customer Service and Disputes: Learn how to provide excellent customer service and address any potential issues that may arise during the dropshipping process.

By the end of this chapter, you'll have a comprehensive understanding of how to harness the power of AliExpress and WooCommerce to create a seamless dropshipping operation. You'll be well on your way to building a profitable online business that leverages the strengths of these two dynamic platforms.

So, let's embark on this exciting journey to integrate AliExpress with WooCommerce and unlock the potential of your dropshipping venture. Get ready to expand your product offerings, automate your processes, and take your online store to new heights of success. Let's dive in!

2.1 Selecting Products to Sell

Your journey in the world of dropshipping starts with a fundamental decision: what products will you offer in your online store? Choosing the right products is a pivotal step that can significantly impact the success of your dropshipping venture. In this section, we will guide you through the process of selecting products to sell, helping you make informed decisions that align with your niche, target audience, and profitability goals.

1. Identify Your Niche

Before diving into product selection, it's essential to define your niche. A niche is a specific market segment or industry that you will focus on. Narrowing down your niche allows you to target a more defined audience and compete effectively in the e-commerce landscape.

Consider factors such as your interests, expertise, and passion when selecting a niche. Your enthusiasm for the niche can translate into better product selection and marketing efforts.

2. Research Market Demand

Once you've identified your niche, research market demand within that niche. You want to offer products that people are actively searching for and interested in purchasing. Here are some research methods:

- Keyword Research: Use tools like Google Keyword Planner or third-party keyword research tools to identify popular search terms related to your niche.

- Competitor Analysis: Study your competitors to see what products they are selling successfully. Analyze their customer reviews and feedback.

- Trend Analysis: Keep an eye on industry trends and consumer preferences. Products that align with current trends may have higher demand.

3. Consider Profit Margins

While it's essential to sell products that are in demand, you must also consider your profit margins.

Research the pricing of potential products and evaluate how much profit you can make after accounting for product costs, shipping fees, and other expenses.

Dropshipping often involves selling products with relatively lower profit margins, so it's crucial to choose a mix of products that balance profitability and demand.

4. Evaluate Supplier Reliability

Since you'll be relying on AliExpress suppliers for your products, it's vital to assess the reliability and reputation of potential suppliers. Look for suppliers with a history of positive reviews and good communication. Check for reliable shipping times and their ability to handle order volume.

5. Product Selection Criteria

Consider the following criteria when selecting products:

- Quality: Choose products that meet or exceed quality expectations. High-quality items lead to satisfied customers and fewer returns.

- Size and Weight: Consider the size and weight of products, as they will impact shipping costs and logistics.

- Shipping Options: Verify that the product can be shipped to your target audience reliably and within a reasonable timeframe.

- Seasonality: Be mindful of seasonal products that may only sell well during specific times of the year.

- Unique Selling Proposition (USP): Identify what sets your products apart from competitors. This could be unique features, superior quality, or competitive pricing.

By following these steps and conducting thorough research, you'll be well-equipped to select products that resonate with your niche, have a solid demand, and offer profit potential. In the upcoming sections, we will explore strategies for sourcing products from AliExpress, managing your inventory, and optimizing product listings to enhance your dropshipping business further.

2.2 Using AliExpress Dropshipping Plugins

As you embark on your journey to create a successful dropshipping business, leveraging the right tools and resources is crucial. One of the key elements that can streamline your dropshipping operations and simplify the process of importing products from AliExpress to your WooCommerce store is the use of AliExpress dropshipping plugins. In this section, we will explore the benefits of these plugins and guide you through the steps to effectively use them to build your product catalog.

1. What Are AliExpress Dropshipping Plugins?

AliExpress dropshipping plugins are software extensions or add-ons that seamlessly integrate with your WooCommerce store. They enable you to import products from AliExpress directly into your store, manage product listings, and automate various aspects of your dropshipping business. These plugins are designed to simplify the process of sourcing and listing products, making your workflow more efficient.

2. Benefits of Using AliExpress Dropshipping Plugins

a. Time Efficiency: These plugins save you significant time by automating product import, update, and order fulfillment processes. You can focus more on growing your business and less on manual tasks.

b. Product Selection: Access a vast selection of products available on AliExpress, giving you the flexibility to curate a diverse product catalog that caters to your target audience.

c. Pricing and Inventory Management: Keep your product prices and inventory levels up-to-date automatically, ensuring accurate information for your customers.

d. Order Fulfillment: Easily process and fulfill customer orders with just a few clicks, reducing the risk of errors and delays.

3. Popular AliExpress Dropshipping Plugins

There are several AliExpress dropshipping plugins available for WooCommerce. Some of the most popular options include:

- AliDropship: A comprehensive solution that offers product import, pricing automation, and order fulfillment features. It also includes a built-in product customization tool.

- Oberlo: A user-friendly plugin that simplifies product import and order processing. It is especially popular among Shopify users but can also be used with WooCommerce.

- Ali2Woo: This plugin provides an array of features for product import, order fulfillment, and inventory management. It is known for its flexibility and customization options.

4. How to Use AliExpress Dropshipping Plugins

Using an AliExpress dropshipping plugin involves several steps:

a. Installation: Install the chosen plugin from the WordPress plugin repository or the developer's website. Follow the installation instructions provided.

b. Configuration: Configure the plugin settings according to your preferences. This includes setting pricing rules, shipping options, and order fulfillment settings.

c. Product Import: Search for and import products from AliExpress into your WooCommerce store using the plugin's interface. You can usually filter products by category, price range, and more.

d. Product Customization: Edit product titles, descriptions, and images to make them unique and appealing to your target audience.

e. Price and Inventory Updates: Set pricing rules and inventory management options to keep your product listings current.

f. Order Fulfillment: When customers place orders on your store, use the plugin to automate order processing and forwarding the order details to AliExpress suppliers.

By effectively using AliExpress dropshipping plugins, you'll streamline your dropshipping operations, offer a wide range of products to your customers, and maintain accurate pricing and inventory information. In the following sections, we'll explore additional strategies for managing your dropshipping business, optimizing product listings, and maximizing your profitability.

Certainly, here's an introduction for section 2.3 of your guide titled "Automating Product Import from AliExpress":

2.3 Automating Product Import from AliExpress

Efficiency is the name of the game in the world of dropshipping. The more streamlined your processes, the more time and energy you can invest in growing your business. One of the key aspects of achieving this efficiency is automating the process of importing products from AliExpress to your WooCommerce store. In this section, we will delve into the strategies and tools that enable you to automate the product import process, saving you valuable time and ensuring your product catalog stays up to date.

1. Benefits of Automating Product Import

a. Time Savings: Manually importing products one by one can be time-consuming and error-prone. Automation eliminates this task, allowing you to focus on other critical aspects of your business.

b. Real-Time Updates: Automated solutions often provide real-time synchronization with AliExpress, ensuring that product information, pricing, and availability are always accurate.

c. Scalability: As your business grows and you want to expand your product catalog, automation becomes even more crucial. It enables you to efficiently handle a larger number of products without increasing your workload significantly.

2. Using AliExpress Dropshipping Plugins

As mentioned in the previous section, AliExpress dropshipping plugins are powerful tools for automating product import. These plugins integrate with your WooCommerce store and provide features like bulk product import, price updates, and inventory management. They also allow you to customize product details to match your branding.

To automate product import using an AliExpress dropshipping plugin:

1. Install and configure your chosen plugin (e.g., AliDropship, Oberlo, Ali2Woo) as per the plugin's instructions.

2. Use the plugin's interface to search for products on AliExpress. You can apply filters to narrow down your search based on criteria like category, price range, and supplier rating.

3. Select the products you want to import to your store and add them to your product catalog.

4. Customize product details, such as titles, descriptions, and images, to make them unique and

appealing to your audience.

5. Set pricing rules and options for price markup, ensuring your prices align with your profit margins.

6. Configure inventory management settings to keep your product availability accurate.

7. Regularly update your product listings to reflect changes on AliExpress, such as price adjustments or product availability.

3. Scheduled Imports

Many AliExpress dropshipping plugins offer scheduled import features. This allows you to set specific times for product updates, ensuring that your product catalog stays fresh without manual intervention. Scheduled imports can be daily, weekly, or at intervals that suit your needs.

4. Bulk Import

Bulk import capabilities are another advantage of using plugins. This feature enables you to add multiple products to your store simultaneously. You can select products from AliExpress and import them to your WooCommerce store with just a few clicks.

5. Monitoring and Alerts

Some plugins provide monitoring and alert features that notify you of changes on AliExpress. For instance, you can receive notifications about price changes or product availability issues, allowing you to take immediate action.

By automating product imports from AliExpress, you'll enhance the efficiency and accuracy of your dropshipping business. This automation ensures that your product catalog is always up to date, enabling you to provide customers with the latest products and pricing. In the following sections, we'll explore strategies for optimizing your product listings, managing inventory, and effectively marketing your dropshipping store.

Certainly, here's an introduction for section 2.4 of your guide titled "Managing AliExpress Orders Efficiently":

2.4 Managing AliExpress Orders Efficiently

As your dropshipping business grows and orders start pouring in, efficient order management becomes paramount. Smoothly handling orders ensures timely delivery to your customers and enhances their satisfaction. In this section, we will discuss strategies and tools for managing AliExpress orders efficiently, allowing you to run your dropshipping business with ease and precision.

1. The Order Fulfillment Process

Before we dive into order management tools and techniques, let's outline the typical order fulfillment process in a dropshipping business:

a. Customer Places an Order: A customer makes a purchase on your WooCommerce store.

b. Order Notification: You receive an order notification through your WooCommerce dashboard or email.

c. Payment Processing: Confirm the payment has been successfully processed.

d. Order Details Sent to AliExpress: Using your chosen dropshipping plugin, the order details (customer name, shipping address, product details, etc.) are automatically sent to the respective AliExpress supplier.

e. Supplier Processes the Order: The AliExpress supplier prepares and ships the product directly to the customer's address.

f. Tracking Information: The supplier provides tracking information, which can be automatically sent to the customer through your store's tracking feature.

g. Customer Receives the Product: The customer receives the product, and the order is marked as completed.

2. Efficient Order Management Techniques

To manage AliExpress orders efficiently, consider the following techniques:

a. Monitor Order Notifications: Regularly check your WooCommerce dashboard and email for order notifications. Promptly acknowledge and process new orders.

b. Automate Order Processing: Use your chosen AliExpress dropshipping plugin to automate the order processing and submission of order details to suppliers. This reduces the risk of errors and saves time.

c. Clear Communication: Maintain open and clear communication with your AliExpress suppliers. If issues arise, address them promptly to avoid delays.

d. Monitor Tracking: Keep an eye on tracking information provided by suppliers. Use the tracking feature in your store to keep customers informed about their order's status.

e. Address Customer Inquiries: Provide excellent customer service by addressing inquiries and concerns promptly. Keep customers informed about any delays or changes to their orders.

f. Consistent Follow-Up: Follow up with customers after they receive their orders to gather feedback and address any potential issues. Happy customers are more likely to become repeat buyers.

3. Tracking and Reporting Tools

Consider using tracking and reporting tools to streamline order management:

a. Order Tracking Tools: WooCommerce offers built-in order tracking features. Additionally, you can explore third-party tracking plugins that provide detailed order tracking information for both you and your customers.

b. Reporting Tools: Utilize reporting tools to monitor the performance of your orders and identify any areas for improvement. WooCommerce offers various reporting options to help you track sales, inventory, and customer behavior.

4. Handling Returns and Refunds

Establish clear return and refund policies to address any issues that may arise. Communicate these policies to your customers and ensure they have a straightforward process for initiating returns or requesting refunds.

Efficient order management is a cornerstone of dropshipping success. By implementing these strategies and using the right tools, you can ensure that your customers receive their orders promptly and enjoy a positive shopping experience. In the upcoming sections, we'll explore techniques for marketing your dropshipping store and scaling your business for long-term success.

Chapter 3: Enhancing Your Store with Essential Plugins

In the world of e-commerce, the key to staying competitive and delivering exceptional customer experiences often lies in the power of plugins. WooCommerce, the robust e-commerce platform powering your online store, is incredibly versatile, but it becomes even more potent when augmented with the right plugins. These extensions add functionality, streamline processes, and help you stand out in the crowded online marketplace.

Welcome to Chapter 3 of "Maximizing Profits with WooCommerce: The Ultimate Guide to Dropshipping from AliExpress." In this chapter, we'll explore the world of essential plugins that can enhance your WooCommerce store and optimize your dropshipping business.

Whether you're new to the world of plugins or a seasoned e-commerce professional, this chapter is a valuable resource. We'll guide you through the selection and installation of plugins that are specifically tailored to boost your dropshipping venture. These plugins cover a wide range of aspects, from automating order processing to optimizing your product listings and improving the overall customer experience.

By the end of this chapter, you'll have a toolkit of essential plugins at your disposal, each designed to address a specific aspect of your dropshipping business. You'll be equipped to:

1. Automate Order Fulfillment: Discover plugins that streamline the process of fulfilling orders, reducing manual tasks and ensuring a smooth and efficient operation.

2. Optimize Product Listings: Learn how to use plugins to enhance your product listings, making them more attractive and engaging to potential customers.

3. Enhance Customer Support: Explore plugins that can help you provide excellent customer service and resolve inquiries and issues promptly.

4. Manage Inventory and Stock: Implement inventory management plugins to keep track of product availability and avoid overselling.

5. Boost SEO and Marketing: Discover tools that can enhance your store's search engine optimization

(SEO) and marketing efforts, helping you attract more visitors and drive sales.

In this chapter, we'll delve into each of these aspects, providing practical guidance on selecting, installing, and configuring essential plugins. We'll also offer insights into how these plugins can benefit your specific dropshipping business, helping you maximize profits and customer satisfaction.

So, whether you're looking to streamline your operations, boost your online visibility, or simply improve the overall shopping experience for your customers, join us on this journey through the world of essential WooCommerce plugins. Let's start enhancing your online store and taking your dropshipping business to the next level. Let's dive in!

3.1 SEO Optimization Tools

In the ever-expanding digital marketplace, visibility is key. To attract potential customers and grow your dropshipping business, you must optimize your online store for search engines. This practice, known as Search Engine Optimization (SEO), involves various strategies and techniques. Fortunately, there are a plethora of SEO optimization tools available to assist you in this endeavor. In this section, we will explore these tools and how to harness their power to improve your store's search engine rankings.

1. The Importance of SEO for Dropshipping

Before delving into SEO optimization tools, it's essential to understand why SEO matters for your dropshipping business:

a. Enhanced Visibility: SEO techniques help your online store rank higher in search engine results pages (SERPs). This increased visibility can drive more organic (unpaid) traffic to your site.

b. Targeted Traffic: Proper SEO optimization ensures that the traffic you attract is relevant to your products and niche, increasing the likelihood of conversions.

c. Competitive Advantage: Effective SEO can give you a competitive edge in the crowded e-commerce landscape, making it easier for potential customers to find your store over competitors.

2. SEO Optimization Tools

Here are some of the most valuable SEO optimization tools available to help you improve your store's search engine rankings:

a. Google Analytics: Google Analytics provides detailed insights into your website's traffic, user behavior, and conversion rates. It helps you understand how users find and interact with your site.

b. Google Search Console: This tool allows you to monitor your website's presence in Google's search results. It provides data on keyword rankings, click-through rates, and any issues that may affect your site's performance.

c. Yoast SEO (WordPress Plugin): If your dropshipping store is built on WordPress, Yoast SEO is a popular plugin that helps you optimize your content for search engines. It offers features like content analysis, XML sitemap generation, and on-page SEO recommendations.

d. Moz: Moz offers a suite of SEO tools, including keyword research, site auditing, and backlink analysis. Their tools can help you identify areas for improvement and track your progress over time.

e. SEMrush: SEMrush is a comprehensive SEO tool that provides insights into keyword rankings, competitor analysis, site audit reports, and more. It's a valuable resource for optimizing your online store and staying competitive.

f. Ahrefs: Ahrefs is known for its robust backlink analysis capabilities. It helps you identify your website's backlinks and analyze the backlink profiles of your competitors. Backlinks play a crucial role in SEO.

g. Screaming Frog SEO Spider: This desktop application crawls your website and provides a detailed analysis of on-page SEO elements, such as titles, meta descriptions, and broken links. It's particularly useful for identifying technical SEO issues.

h. Ubersuggest: Ubersuggest is a free SEO tool that offers keyword research, content ideas, and site audit reports. It's a great starting point for beginners looking to improve their SEO.

3. Implementing SEO Strategies

While SEO optimization tools are valuable, it's important to note that SEO is an ongoing process. Here are some key SEO strategies to consider:

- Keyword Research: Identify relevant keywords and phrases that your target audience is likely to use when searching for products in your niche.

- On-Page SEO: Optimize your product listings and content with keyword-rich titles, meta descriptions, and high-quality images.

- Quality Content: Create informative, engaging, and valuable content that resonates with your audience and encourages sharing.

- Link Building: Build high-quality backlinks to your website through guest posting, influencer outreach, and content marketing.

- Mobile Optimization: Ensure your website is mobile-friendly, as Google prioritizes mobile-friendly sites in its rankings.

- Site Speed: Improve your website's loading speed, as faster sites tend to rank higher in search results.

By combining the power of SEO optimization tools with these strategies, you can boost your store's search engine rankings, attract more organic traffic, and ultimately, increase your dropshipping business's success. In the upcoming sections, we'll explore additional techniques for marketing your dropshipping store and expanding your customer base.

3.2 Payment Gateway Integrations

A seamless and secure payment process is fundamental to the success of your dropshipping business. Payment gateway integrations play a crucial role in facilitating transactions on your e-commerce store. In this section, we will explore the importance of payment gateways and how to integrate them into your online store for smooth and secure payment processing.

1. The Significance of Payment Gateways

Payment gateways are the digital bridges that connect your online store with financial institutions, allowing you to accept payments from customers. Choosing the right payment gateway is essential for several reasons:

a. Customer Trust: A reputable payment gateway instills confidence in your customers, assuring them that their financial information is secure during transactions.

b. Global Accessibility: Payment gateways enable you to accept payments from customers worldwide, expanding your reach and potential customer base.

c. Convenience: They provide a convenient and efficient payment process for both you and your customers, reducing friction in the buying process.

d. Security: Reliable payment gateways incorporate advanced security measures to protect sensitive financial data, reducing the risk of fraud.

2. Popular Payment Gateways for Dropshipping

When selecting payment gateways for your dropshipping store, consider the following popular options:

a. PayPal: PayPal is a widely recognized and trusted payment gateway that supports both credit card payments and PayPal account payments. It's known for its user-friendly interface and global reach.

b. Stripe: Stripe is a robust payment gateway that offers customizable options, supports a variety of payment methods, and provides advanced fraud prevention tools. It's known for its developer-friendly approach.

c. Square: Square is a versatile payment gateway that seamlessly integrates with your store. It's a great option for businesses that want to accept in-person payments along with online transactions.

d. Authorize.Net: Authorize.Net is a long-established payment gateway known for its reliability and security features. It supports a wide range of payment methods and offers advanced fraud detection tools.

e. 2Checkout (now Verifone): 2Checkout, rebranded as Verifone, is a global payment gateway that enables you to accept payments in multiple currencies and languages. It's ideal for businesses with international customers.

f. Braintree: Braintree, a subsidiary of PayPal, offers a seamless and secure payment experience. It's known for its ease of use and developer-friendly features.

3. Integrating Payment Gateways with WooCommerce

To integrate payment gateways into your WooCommerce store:

a. Choose a Payment Gateway: Select the payment gateway(s) that align with your business needs and customer preferences. Ensure it supports the currencies and regions you plan to serve.

b. Install the Plugin: Most payment gateways offer WooCommerce plugins that simplify the integration process. Install the plugin from your WordPress dashboard and follow the setup instructions provided by the payment gateway provider.

c. Configure Payment Settings: In your WooCommerce settings, configure the payment gateway's settings, including API keys, account details, and other necessary information.

d. Test Transactions: Before going live, conduct test transactions to ensure that payments are processed correctly, and funds are transferred to your account as expected.

e. Offer Multiple Payment Options: Consider offering multiple payment options to accommodate a broader range of customer preferences. This can include credit cards, digital wallets, and alternative payment methods.

f. Ensure Security: Implement robust security measures to protect customer payment data. Use SSL certificates and stay compliant with industry standards, such as PCI DSS (Payment Card Industry Data Security Standard).

Integrating payment gateways into your dropshipping store enhances the customer experience, builds trust, and enables you to efficiently process transactions. By offering a variety of payment options, you cater to diverse customer needs and increase the likelihood of completed purchases. In the following sections, we'll delve into marketing strategies and scaling techniques to further grow your dropshipping business.

3.3 Advanced Analytics Plugins

In the fast-paced world of e-commerce, data is king. To make informed decisions, optimize your strategies, and drive growth for your dropshipping business, you need access to comprehensive analytics. Advanced analytics plugins are valuable tools that can provide you with insights into your store's performance, customer behavior, and marketing effectiveness. In this section, we will explore the significance of advanced analytics and how to harness the power of these plugins to elevate your business.

1. The Role of Analytics in Dropshipping

Analytics serve as the eyes and ears of your dropshipping business. They allow you to:

a. Monitor Performance: Track the performance of your online store, including sales, traffic, and conversion rates.

b. Understand Customer Behavior: Gain insights into how customers interact with your website, which products they prefer, and their journey from landing on your site to making a purchase.

c. Optimize Marketing: Evaluate the effectiveness of your marketing campaigns, including advertising, email marketing, and social media efforts.

d. Identify Opportunities: Identify trends and opportunities for growth, such as emerging product categories or untapped customer segments.

2. Benefits of Advanced Analytics Plugins

Here are some of the key benefits of utilizing advanced analytics plugins for your dropshipping business:

a. Real-Time Data: Most advanced analytics plugins provide real-time data, enabling you to stay up to date with the latest insights and make timely decisions.

b. Customization: Tailor your analytics to focus on the metrics that matter most to your business goals, whether it's sales, customer engagement, or traffic sources.

c. Conversion Tracking: Monitor the entire customer journey, from the moment users land on your site to when they make a purchase or abandon their cart.

d. Performance Benchmarking: Compare your store's performance over time and against industry benchmarks to identify areas for improvement.

e. Marketing Insights: Assess the ROI of your marketing efforts and allocate resources to the most effective channels and campaigns.

3. Popular Advanced Analytics Plugins

Consider incorporating the following advanced analytics plugins into your WooCommerce store:

a. Google Analytics: Google Analytics is a versatile and widely used analytics platform. By integrating it with your store, you can access in-depth data on user behavior, conversion rates, and traffic sources.

b. MonsterInsights: MonsterInsights is a popular Google Analytics plugin for WordPress. It simplifies the integration process and offers additional features like e-commerce tracking and event tracking.

c. Metorik: Metorik is a powerful WooCommerce analytics and management tool that provides advanced reporting, customer insights, and segmentation options. It's designed specifically for WooCommerce users.

d. Mixpanel: Mixpanel is an analytics platform that focuses on user-centric analytics. It helps you understand how individual users interact with your store and products.

e. Hotjar: Hotjar offers behavior analytics and feedback tools, including heatmaps, session recordings, and surveys. It helps you visualize how users engage with your website.

f. Kissmetrics: Kissmetrics is a customer analytics and engagement platform that provides insights into user journeys and customer retention. It helps you identify areas for improving user experience.

4. Implementing Analytics Strategies

To maximize the benefits of advanced analytics plugins:

a. Set Clear Goals: Define specific goals and objectives for your analytics efforts. What do you want to achieve, and which metrics will help you measure progress?

b. Regularly Review Data: Make it a habit to regularly review your analytics data to spot trends, anomalies, and areas for improvement.

c. A/B Testing: Use A/B testing to experiment with different strategies and measure their impact on key metrics.

d. Customer Segmentation: Segment your customer base to gain insights into different audience groups and tailor your marketing efforts accordingly.

e. Continuous Learning: Stay updated on industry trends and changes in analytics platforms to make the most of your data.

By leveraging advanced analytics plugins, you'll gain valuable insights into your dropshipping business's performance, enabling you to make data-driven decisions that drive growth and enhance the overall customer experience. In the following sections, we'll explore marketing tactics, customer engagement strategies, and scaling techniques to further expand your dropshipping venture.

3.4 Email Marketing and Automation Tools

Email marketing remains one of the most powerful and cost-effective methods for engaging customers, driving sales, and nurturing long-lasting relationships. Email marketing and automation tools are essential assets for any dropshipping business looking to connect with its audience effectively. In this section, we will explore the significance of email marketing, and how to utilize automation tools to streamline your efforts and boost your business.

1. The Role of Email Marketing

Email marketing plays a multifaceted role in the success of your dropshipping business:

a. Customer Retention: It helps you nurture existing customer relationships, encouraging repeat purchases and brand loyalty.

b. Customer Acquisition: Email campaigns can attract new customers and subscribers, expanding your customer base.

c. Promotion and Sales: You can promote products, offer discounts, and drive sales through strategically timed email campaigns.

d. Personalization: Email allows for personalization, delivering tailored content and offers based on customer preferences and behavior.

e. Automation: Automation tools streamline repetitive tasks, such as sending welcome emails, abandoned cart reminders, and order confirmations.

2. Benefits of Email Marketing and Automation

Here are some key benefits of incorporating email marketing and automation into your dropshipping strategy:

a. Time Efficiency: Automation tools handle routine email tasks, freeing up your time for other aspects of your business.

b. Targeted Marketing: Segment your email list to send highly relevant content and offers to different customer groups.

c. Increased Sales: Well-crafted email campaigns can drive sales and boost revenue, especially during promotional periods.

d. Data-Driven Insights: Email analytics provide valuable insights into the effectiveness of your campaigns, allowing you to refine your strategies.

e. Customer Engagement: Regular email communication keeps your brand top-of-mind and fosters ongoing engagement with your audience.

3. Popular Email Marketing and Automation Tools

Consider utilizing the following email marketing and automation tools to enhance your dropshipping business:

a. Mailchimp: Mailchimp is a user-friendly email marketing platform that offers automation features, customizable templates, and detailed analytics.

b. Klaviyo: Klaviyo is designed for e-commerce businesses and specializes in email automation, segmentation, and personalized messaging.

c. ConvertKit: ConvertKit is a robust email marketing tool that caters to bloggers, content creators, and small businesses. It offers advanced automation and segmentation capabilities.

d. Omnisend: Omnisend is an omnichannel marketing automation platform that specializes in email and SMS marketing for e-commerce. It includes automation workflows and audience segmentation.

e. ActiveCampaign: ActiveCampaign is an all-in-one marketing automation platform that combines email marketing with CRM features, making it suitable for advanced automation and customer relationship management.

f. Drip: Drip is an e-commerce CRM and marketing automation platform that focuses on personalization and customer journey automation.

4. Implementing Email Marketing Strategies

To make the most of email marketing and automation tools:

a. Build an Email List: Encourage website visitors to subscribe to your email list through sign-up forms and incentives like discounts or newsletters.

b. Segment Your List: Divide your email list into segments based on customer behavior, demographics, or purchase history. Send targeted campaigns to each segment.

c. Create Engaging Content: Craft compelling email content, including product recommendations, promotional offers, and valuable information.

d. Automate Workflows: Set up automation workflows for tasks like welcoming new subscribers, recovering abandoned carts, and post-purchase follow-ups.

e. Monitor and Analyze: Regularly review email analytics to assess the performance of your campaigns. Adjust your strategies based on what works best.

Email marketing and automation tools are indispensable for effectively engaging customers, driving sales, and building brand loyalty. By harnessing the power of email marketing, you can stay connected with your audience and nurture long-term customer relationships. In the upcoming sections, we'll explore additional marketing tactics, customer service strategies, and tips for scaling your dropshipping business to new heights.

Chapter 4: Mastering Dropshipping Operations

Congratulations on reaching Chapter 4 of "Maximizing Profits with WooCommerce: The Ultimate Guide to Dropshipping from AliExpress." By now, you've set up your online store, integrated AliExpress with WooCommerce, and enhanced your store's capabilities with essential plugins. You're well on your way to establishing a successful dropshipping venture.

In this chapter, we'll delve deep into the operational aspects of your dropshipping business. Mastering dropshipping operations is essential for running a smooth, efficient, and profitable online store. We'll guide you through the various facets of day-to-day management, automation, and optimization to help you stay ahead in the competitive e-commerce landscape.

Here's what you can expect to explore in this chapter:

1. Effective Supplier Management: Discover strategies for managing your relationships with AliExpress suppliers. Learn how to communicate effectively, ensure product quality, and resolve any potential issues.

2. Order Processing Automation: Explore advanced techniques and tools for automating order processing. This includes methods for order placement, tracking, and managing returns or refunds.

3. Inventory and Stock Control: Gain insights into maintaining accurate inventory levels to prevent overselling or running out of stock. We'll also discuss strategies for handling backorders and managing product discontinuations.

4. Customer Service Excellence: Learn how to provide outstanding customer service to build trust and loyalty among your customers. We'll cover handling inquiries, returns, and addressing customer

concerns effectively.

5. Scaling Your Business: Explore strategies for scaling your dropshipping business, from expanding your product catalog to optimizing your operations for growth.

6. Profit Maximization: Discover techniques for increasing your profitability, including setting competitive prices, managing shipping costs, and identifying cost-saving opportunities.

Throughout this chapter, we'll provide practical tips, best practices, and real-world examples to illustrate how to navigate the intricacies of dropshipping operations effectively. Whether you're running a small dropshipping store or aiming for substantial growth, the insights in this chapter will help you master the day-to-day operations of your business.

As you progress through this chapter, you'll become better equipped to handle the challenges and opportunities that come with running a dropshipping business. By implementing the strategies and techniques discussed here, you'll be well on your way to maximizing your profits and ensuring the long-term success of your online store.

So, let's dive into the world of dropshipping operations, fine-tuning your processes, and taking your business to new heights. Get ready to master the art of efficient and profitable dropshipping. Let's begin!

4.1 Inventory Management Strategies

As your dropshipping business grows, efficient inventory management becomes increasingly vital. Properly managing your inventory ensures that you can fulfill customer orders promptly, prevent stockouts, and maximize profitability. In this section, we will explore essential inventory management strategies to help you scale your dropshipping business effectively.

1. The Significance of Inventory Management

Effective inventory management offers several crucial benefits for your dropshipping business:

a. Customer Satisfaction: Timely order fulfillment leads to satisfied customers who are more likely to return for future purchases.

b. Cost Efficiency: Efficient inventory management helps reduce storage costs, overstocking expenses, and the risk of obsolete inventory.

c. Profitability: By optimizing your inventory levels, you can maximize profit margins and minimize losses associated with carrying excess stock.

d. Scalability: A well-organized inventory system is essential for scaling your business without disruptions.

2. Inventory Management Strategies

Here are key inventory management strategies to consider for your dropshipping business:

a. Regular Audits: Conduct regular audits of your inventory to track the quantity, condition, and value of your products. This ensures accuracy and helps prevent discrepancies.

b. Demand Forecasting: Use historical sales data, market trends, and seasonality to forecast future demand for your products. Accurate forecasting allows you to adjust inventory levels proactively.

c. Safety Stock: Maintain a safety stock buffer for high-demand items or products with long lead times. This buffer helps prevent stockouts during unexpected surges in demand or shipping delays.

d. Vendor Relationships: Cultivate strong relationships with your AliExpress suppliers. Good communication and reliability from your suppliers can help you manage inventory effectively.

e. Order Management: Implement an automated order management system that tracks orders, updates inventory levels, and communicates with your suppliers seamlessly.

f. Dropshipping Software: Utilize dropshipping software and plugins that offer real-time inventory tracking and automatic order placement with suppliers.

g. Inventory Categories: Categorize your products based on their sales velocity. High-velocity items may require more frequent restocking, while low-velocity items can be managed differently.

h. ABC Analysis: Apply the ABC analysis method to classify products into three categories: A (high-value, low-quantity), B (moderate-value, moderate-quantity), and C (low-value, high-quantity). Allocate resources and attention accordingly.

i. Economic Order Quantity (EOQ): Calculate the EOQ for your products to determine the optimal order quantity that minimizes costs while maintaining inventory levels.

j. Just-In-Time (JIT): Consider implementing a just-in-time inventory system, which aims to keep minimal stock on hand and relies on timely deliveries from suppliers.

k. Seasonal Adjustments: Adjust your inventory strategies to accommodate seasonal fluctuations in demand. Stock up on seasonal products well in advance to meet customer needs.

l. Inventory Alerts: Set up inventory alerts to notify you when stock levels drop below a certain threshold. This ensures you can reorder in a timely manner.

3. Inventory Management Tools

Explore inventory management tools and software to streamline your operations:

a. Inventory Management Software: Consider using dedicated inventory management software like TradeGecko, Zoho Inventory, or Skubana, which can centralize inventory data and automate various tasks.

b. Spreadsheets: Excel or Google Sheets can be used for basic inventory tracking, especially if you have a smaller product catalog.

c. E-commerce Platforms: Many e-commerce platforms, including WooCommerce, offer inventory management features that integrate seamlessly with your online store.

d. Dropshipping Plugins: Some AliExpress dropshipping plugins also provide inventory tracking and order management features to help you monitor stock levels.

Effective inventory management is essential for the long-term success and scalability of your dropshipping business. By implementing these strategies and utilizing inventory management tools, you can maintain a well-organized and efficient inventory system, ensuring that you can meet customer demand while minimizing costs and risks. In the following sections, we'll explore additional scaling strategies, marketing tactics, and customer service enhancements to take your dropshipping business to the next level.

4.2 Handling Shipping and Delivery

Efficient shipping and delivery management are integral components of a successful dropshipping business. Providing timely and reliable delivery services not only enhances customer satisfaction but also contributes to your brand's reputation. In this section, we will explore essential strategies for handling shipping and delivery as your dropshipping business scales.

1. The Importance of Shipping and Delivery

Shipping and delivery are the tangible aspects of your dropshipping business that directly impact your customers' experience:

a. Customer Expectations: Today's customers expect quick and reliable delivery services. Meeting or exceeding these expectations is crucial for retaining and attracting customers.

b. Brand Reputation: Efficient shipping and delivery contribute to a positive brand reputation, encouraging word-of-mouth referrals and repeat business.

c. Competitive Advantage: Offering competitive shipping options and faster delivery times can give you an edge over competitors.

d. Operational Efficiency: Streamlined shipping and delivery processes improve overall operational efficiency, reducing costs and potential errors.

2. Shipping and Delivery Strategies

Here are key shipping and delivery strategies to consider as you scale your dropshipping business:

a. Diverse Shipping Options: Offer a range of shipping options to accommodate varying customer preferences, including standard, expedited, and international shipping.

b. Shipping Cost Transparency: Clearly communicate shipping costs to customers at checkout. Consider offering free shipping for orders over a certain threshold to incentivize larger purchases.

c. Shipping Time Estimates: Provide accurate delivery time estimates to manage customer expectations. This includes displaying estimated delivery dates during the checkout process.

d. Tracking and Notifications: Implement a robust tracking system that allows customers to monitor the progress of their orders. Send automated shipping notifications and tracking information to keep customers informed.

e. Shipping Partners: Establish relationships with reliable shipping carriers or fulfillment centers that can consistently deliver products on time. Evaluate carrier performance and consider multiple shipping partners to ensure redundancy.

f. Returns and Refunds: Have clear policies and procedures in place for handling returns and refunds. Make it easy for customers to initiate returns and track the status of their requests.

g. International Shipping: If you plan to expand internationally, research and understand the customs and import regulations of target countries. Offer international shipping options while addressing potential customs delays.

h. Inventory and Location: Consider strategically locating inventory in different regions to reduce shipping distances and improve delivery times.

i. Packaging: Use appropriate and secure packaging to protect products during transit. Consider eco-friendly packaging options to align with sustainability goals.

j. Third-Party Shipping Software: Invest in shipping software or plugins that integrate with your e-commerce platform to streamline label printing, order processing, and carrier selection.

3. Shipping Costs and Pricing

Managing shipping costs is critical to maintaining profitability:

a. Price Optimization: Factor shipping costs into your product pricing strategy. Be transparent with customers about shipping fees.

b. Negotiate Rates: Negotiate shipping rates with carriers, especially if you anticipate high shipping volumes as your business grows.

c. Shipping Discounts: Explore shipping discounts and partnerships offered by e-commerce platforms, shipping carriers, or third-party shipping solutions.

d. Shipping Zones: Implement a shipping zone strategy to calculate shipping costs based on distance or location. Adjust pricing accordingly.

4. Shipping and Delivery Automation

Consider automating various aspects of shipping and delivery, such as:

a. Label Printing: Use shipping software to generate shipping labels, reducing manual data entry.

b. Order Tracking: Implement automated order tracking and notifications to keep customers informed.

c. Inventory Updates: Automate inventory updates to ensure accurate stock levels on your website.

Efficient shipping and delivery management are essential for the growth and success of your dropshipping business. By implementing these strategies and leveraging automation tools, you can provide an exceptional customer experience, reduce operational challenges, and position your brand as a reliable and efficient provider in the competitive e-commerce landscape. In the following sections, we'll explore additional scaling techniques, marketing strategies, and customer service enhancements to further elevate your dropshipping venture.

4.3 Dealing with Returns and Refunds

Returns and refunds are an inevitable part of the e-commerce landscape, and how you handle them can greatly impact your dropshipping business's reputation and customer satisfaction. As your business scales, it's essential to have effective processes in place for managing returns and issuing refunds. In this section, we will explore the importance of handling returns and refunds professionally and provide strategies to streamline this aspect of your business.

1. The Significance of Returns and Refunds

Returns and refunds are a common occurrence in e-commerce for various reasons:

a. Customer Expectations: Customers expect a hassle-free return and refund process when they encounter issues with their orders.

b. Customer Retention: Handling returns and refunds well can turn dissatisfied customers into loyal ones, as it demonstrates excellent customer service.

c. Legal Obligations: Complying with consumer protection laws and regulations is crucial to avoid legal complications.

d. Reputation Management: A well-handled return or refund request can enhance your brand's reputation, while mishandling them can harm it.

2. Returns and Refund Strategies

Here are key strategies for managing returns and refunds as your dropshipping business scales:

a. Clear Return Policy: Have a clear and concise return policy that is easily accessible on your website. It should outline the conditions for returns, including timeframes, acceptable reasons, and the process to initiate a return.

b. Streamlined Return Process: Implement a user-friendly return process that allows customers to initiate returns online. Provide a return authorization (RA) number or label for easy tracking.

c. Return Shipping: Clearly communicate who is responsible for return shipping costs, whether it's the customer, your business, or the supplier. Offering prepaid return labels can simplify the process for customers.

d. Refund Timelines: Specify the timeframe within which refunds will be processed and issued. Aim to process refunds promptly, ideally within a few business days of receiving returned items.

e. Tracking Returns: Implement a system to track returned items to ensure they are received and inspected in a timely manner.

f. Inspection and Restocking: Thoroughly inspect returned items for damage or signs of use. Consider restocking returned items that are in good condition.

g. Refund Options: Provide customers with options for refunds, such as returning funds to their original payment method, store credit, or exchanges.

h. Customer Communication: Keep customers informed at each step of the return and refund process. Send automated emails to confirm return initiation, receipt of returned items, and refund issuance.

i. Record Keeping: Maintain detailed records of return and refund transactions for accounting and compliance purposes.

j. Monitor Return Trends: Analyze return data to identify trends or patterns. This can help you address recurring issues, such as product quality or sizing concerns.

3. Handling Refund Disputes

Occasionally, customers may dispute refund decisions. Have a protocol in place to address these disputes, including clear communication channels and a process for escalating issues if necessary.

4. Continual Improvement

Continually assess and improve your return and refund processes based on customer feedback and data analysis. Seek opportunities to reduce return rates by addressing common issues at their root cause.

5. Legal Compliance

Ensure that your return and refund policies comply with applicable consumer protection laws and regulations in the regions where you operate. Consult with legal professionals if needed to stay compliant.

Handling returns and refunds professionally and efficiently is crucial for maintaining customer trust and building a strong brand reputation as your dropshipping business grows. By implementing clear policies and streamlined processes, you can navigate these challenges with confidence and maintain a positive relationship with your customers. In the following sections, we'll explore additional scaling techniques, marketing strategies, and customer service enhancements to further elevate your dropshipping venture.

4.4 Providing Excellent Customer Service

Exceptional customer service is the cornerstone of a successful dropshipping business. As your business scales, maintaining a high level of customer satisfaction becomes even more crucial. In this section, we will explore the significance of excellent customer service and provide strategies to ensure your customers receive the support they need.

1. The Importance of Excellent Customer Service

Customer service goes beyond resolving issues—it's about creating positive experiences and building lasting relationships with your customers:

a. Customer Loyalty: Outstanding service fosters customer loyalty, leading to repeat purchases and referrals.

b. Brand Reputation: Happy customers are more likely to leave positive reviews and recommendations, enhancing your brand's reputation.

c. Competitive Advantage: Superior customer service can set you apart from competitors and encourage customers to choose your store.

d. Issue Resolution: Efficiently resolving customer inquiries and issues helps maintain trust and prevents negative feedback.

2. Strategies for Excellent Customer Service

Here are key strategies for providing excellent customer service as your dropshipping business scales:

a. Responsive Communication: Respond to customer inquiries, emails, and messages promptly. Set clear expectations for response times and availability.

b. Knowledgeable Support: Equip your customer support team with comprehensive knowledge about your products, policies, and procedures.

c. Self-Service Resources: Create a robust FAQ section and knowledge base on your website to empower customers to find answers to common questions independently.

d. Multichannel Support: Offer customer support through multiple channels, including email, live chat, social media, and phone support, to accommodate diverse customer preferences.

e. Personalization: Address customers by their names and tailor responses to their specific inquiries or issues.

f. Handling Complaints: Train your team to handle customer complaints and issues professionally and empathetically. Aim to resolve issues to the customer's satisfaction.

g. Customer Feedback: Actively seek and value customer feedback. Use feedback to identify areas for improvement and make necessary adjustments.

h. Post-Purchase Follow-Up: Send post-purchase follow-up emails to inquire about the customer's experience and offer assistance if needed.

i. Quality Assurance: Conduct quality checks to ensure that products are accurately described, packaged securely, and shipped on time to minimize issues.

j. Escalation Process: Establish an escalation process for complex issues that require higher-level intervention.

k. Training and Development: Invest in ongoing training and development for your customer support team to keep them updated and motivated.

l. 24/7 Support: If feasible, offer 24/7 customer support or extended hours to cater to customers in different time zones.

3. Customer Feedback and Surveys

Regularly collect customer feedback through surveys, reviews, and ratings. Use this feedback to make improvements to your products, services, and customer support processes.

4. Performance Metrics

Monitor key performance metrics related to customer service, such as response times, resolution rates, and customer satisfaction scores. Use data to evaluate the effectiveness of your customer support efforts.

5. Automation and AI

Consider implementing chatbots and AI-powered customer service tools to handle routine inquiries and provide immediate responses, freeing up your human support team for more complex issues.

6. Training and Empowerment

Empower your customer support team to make decisions and resolve issues independently. Provide ongoing training to ensure they have the skills and knowledge needed to excel in their roles.

Providing excellent customer service is an ongoing commitment that can greatly impact the success and growth of your dropshipping business. By prioritizing customer satisfaction, you can create loyal customers who not only return for repeat business but also become advocates for your brand. In the following sections, we'll explore additional scaling techniques, marketing strategies, and operational enhancements to further elevate your dropshipping venture.

Chapter 5: Marketing Your Dropshipping Store

Welcome to the fifth chapter of "Maximizing Profits with WooCommerce: The Ultimate Guide to Dropshipping from AliExpress." By now, you've established a solid foundation for your dropshipping business, mastered the intricacies of operations, and fine-tuned your online store. Now it's time to focus on spreading the word and driving customers to your virtual storefront.

In this chapter, we'll dive into the world of marketing, exploring strategies and tactics to promote your dropshipping store effectively. Marketing is the engine that powers your business, helping you attract, engage, and convert potential customers into loyal buyers. Whether you're new to marketing or looking to refine your existing strategies, this chapter will equip you with the knowledge and tools needed to succeed.

Here's what you can expect to explore in this chapter:

1. Creating a Marketing Plan: Understand the importance of a well-structured marketing plan and how to develop one tailored to your dropshipping business. We'll cover market research, target audience identification, and goal setting.

2. Content Marketing: Learn how to leverage the power of content to attract and engage your audience. We'll discuss blog posts, product descriptions, and other types of content that can drive traffic and enhance your brand's credibility.

3. Search Engine Optimization (SEO): Discover the principles of SEO and how to optimize your website for better visibility in search engine results. Improve your chances of ranking higher and attracting organic traffic.

4. Social Media Marketing: Explore strategies for effectively using social media platforms to connect with your audience, build a community, and promote your products. We'll cover platforms like Facebook, Instagram, and Pinterest.

5. Email Marketing: Harness the potential of email marketing to nurture leads, engage customers, and drive sales. We'll discuss best practices for building and maintaining an email list and creating compelling email campaigns.

6. Paid Advertising: Learn about pay-per-click (PPC) advertising and how to run effective paid ad campaigns on platforms like Google Ads and Facebook Ads. Discover how to set budgets, target audiences, and measure campaign success.

7. Influencer Marketing: Explore the world of influencer marketing and how partnering with influencers can boost your brand's visibility and credibility.

8. Analytics and Monitoring: Understand the importance of data-driven decision-making and how to use analytics tools to measure the effectiveness of your marketing efforts.

Throughout this chapter, we'll provide practical tips, real-world examples, and actionable strategies to help you market your dropshipping store effectively. Marketing is an ongoing process, and the insights you gain here will empower you to adapt and refine your strategies as your business evolves.

By the end of this chapter, you'll have a comprehensive understanding of how to promote your dropshipping store, drive traffic, and increase sales. Let's dive into the exciting world of marketing and take your dropshipping business to new heights. Let's get started!

5.1 Developing a Strong Brand Identity

A strong brand identity is the bedrock of any successful dropshipping business. As your business scales, it becomes increasingly important to establish a memorable and consistent brand identity that resonates with your target audience. In this section, we will explore the significance of brand identity and provide strategies to develop and maintain a strong brand presence.

1. The Power of Brand Identity

Brand identity encompasses the visual and emotional elements that define your business and set it apart from competitors:

a. Recognition: A strong brand identity makes your business easily recognizable, even in a crowded market.

b. Trust: Consistency in branding builds trust with customers, assuring them of the quality and reliability of your products and services.

c. Customer Loyalty: A compelling brand identity can foster customer loyalty, encouraging repeat purchases and advocacy.

d. Differentiation: A unique brand identity helps your business stand out among competitors, making it easier for customers to choose your store.

2. Strategies for Developing a Strong Brand Identity

Here are key strategies for developing a strong brand identity as your dropshipping business scales:

a. Define Your Brand: Begin by defining your brand's mission, values, and personality. What does your business stand for, and what sets it apart?

b. Target Audience: Understand your target audience's preferences, needs, and pain points. Tailor your brand identity to resonate with them.

c. Brand Name and Logo: Choose a memorable brand name and design a distinctive logo that reflects your brand's essence.

d. Visual Identity: Develop a consistent visual identity, including color schemes, typography, and design elements, to use across all brand materials.

e. Brand Voice: Establish a unique brand voice that reflects your brand's personality and speaks to your audience. Consistency in tone and messaging is crucial.

f. Brand Storytelling: Craft a compelling brand story that connects with customers emotionally. Share your journey, values, and the problem your business solves.

g. Consistency: Ensure that your brand identity is consistently applied across all touchpoints, from your website and social media to packaging and customer interactions.

h. Customer Experience: Create a positive and memorable customer experience that aligns with your brand identity. This includes everything from website navigation to post-purchase interactions.

i. Testimonials and Social Proof: Showcase customer reviews, testimonials, and social proof to build credibility and trust.

j. Adaptability: As your business evolves, your brand identity may need adjustments to stay relevant and resonate with changing market dynamics.

3. Brand Guidelines

Develop comprehensive brand guidelines that detail your brand's visual and verbal elements. These guidelines ensure consistency and serve as a reference for anyone involved in brand-related tasks.

4. Brand Refresh or Rebrand

Consider the possibility of a brand refresh or rebrand if your business undergoes significant changes or if you want to breathe new life into your brand identity.

5. Market Research

Regularly conduct market research to stay informed about industry trends, customer preferences, and competitive positioning. Use insights from research to fine-tune your brand identity.

6. Brand Storytelling

Craft compelling brand stories that connect with customers on an emotional level. Share stories about your products, the people behind your brand, and the impact your business makes.

7. Brand Evangelism

Encourage brand evangelism by cultivating a community of loyal customers who advocate for your brand. Reward and engage with your most passionate supporters.

Developing and nurturing a strong brand identity is an ongoing process that can significantly impact the success and growth of your dropshipping business. By consistently and authentically representing your brand, you can build trust, loyalty, and recognition within your target audience. In the following sections, we'll explore additional strategies for establishing a strong online presence, marketing effectively, and scaling your dropshipping venture further.

5.2 Effective Social Media Strategies

Social media has evolved into a powerful tool for connecting with your audience, building brand awareness, and driving sales in the world of e-commerce. As your dropshipping business scales, implementing effective social media strategies becomes crucial for expanding your reach and engaging with customers. In this section, we will explore the significance of social media marketing and provide strategies to harness its potential for your brand.

1. The Power of Social Media

Social media platforms offer numerous benefits for your dropshipping business:

a. Brand Visibility: Social media helps you increase your brand's visibility and reach a broader audience.

b. Audience Engagement: Engage with your audience through posts, comments, and direct messages, fostering a sense of community.

c. Product Promotion: Promote your products, run targeted ad campaigns, and showcase your offerings to potential customers.

d. Customer Feedback: Receive real-time feedback from customers and address their inquiries and concerns.

e. Content Sharing: Share valuable content, such as blog posts, videos, and tutorials, to establish authority in your niche.

f. Influencer Partnerships: Collaborate with influencers and bloggers to extend your brand's reach to their followers.

g. Data Insights: Utilize social media analytics to understand your audience's preferences and track the performance of your campaigns.

2. Strategies for Effective Social Media Marketing

Here are key strategies to develop effective social media marketing as your dropshipping business scales:

a. Platform Selection: Identify the social media platforms that align with your target audience and business goals. Common platforms include Facebook, Instagram, Twitter, Pinterest, and TikTok.

b. Content Planning: Create a content calendar that outlines your posting schedule and content types. Include a mix of product highlights, educational content, customer stories, and promotional posts.

c. Visual Branding: Maintain consistent visual branding across your social media profiles to reinforce your brand identity. Use high-quality images and graphics.

d. Engagement Strategy: Respond promptly to comments, messages, and mentions. Encourage discussions and interaction by asking questions and running polls.

e. Influencer Marketing: Partner with influencers in your niche who can authentically promote your products to their followers.

f. Paid Advertising: Utilize paid social media advertising to reach specific demographics, retarget website visitors, and promote seasonal or special offers.

g. User-Generated Content: Encourage customers to share their experiences with your products by featuring user-generated content on your social media profiles.

h. Hashtag Usage: Research and use relevant hashtags to expand the reach of your posts and make them discoverable to a broader audience.

i. Analytics and Optimization: Regularly review social media analytics to assess the performance of your posts and campaigns. Adjust your strategies based on data insights.

j. Cross-Promotion: Cross-promote your social media accounts on your website, email newsletters, and other marketing channels to increase your following.

k. Customer Stories: Share customer success stories and testimonials to build trust and credibility.

l. Seasonal Campaigns: Plan and execute seasonal or holiday-themed social media campaigns to capitalize on festive shopping trends.

3. Content Creation

Invest in high-quality content creation, including visually appealing images, engaging videos, informative blog posts, and captivating captions. Consistently share content that resonates with your audience.

4. Social Media Management Tools

Explore social media management tools and scheduling platforms that can help you streamline your posting and analytics tracking across multiple platforms.

5. Community Building

Build a loyal community around your brand by fostering meaningful connections, responding to feedback, and actively participating in discussions related to your niche.

6. Consistency

Consistency in posting, branding, and engagement is key to maintaining a strong and active social media presence.

Effective social media strategies can help you connect with your audience, drive sales, and build a loyal customer base as your dropshipping business scales. By implementing these strategies and staying attuned to the preferences and feedback of your audience, you can leverage the full potential of social media marketing. In the following sections, we'll explore additional methods to enhance your online presence, expand your marketing efforts, and scale your dropshipping venture further.

5.3 Leveraging Email Marketing

Email marketing remains a powerful and cost-effective tool for engaging your audience, nurturing customer relationships, and driving sales. As your dropshipping business scales, email marketing can become a central component of your marketing strategy. In this section, we will explore the significance of email marketing and provide strategies to leverage its potential for your brand.

1. The Power of Email Marketing

Email marketing offers numerous advantages for your dropshipping business:

a. Direct Communication: Email provides a direct and personalized channel for communicating with your audience.

b. Customer Retention: Nurture existing customer relationships, encourage repeat purchases, and foster brand loyalty.

c. Customer Acquisition: Attract new customers and subscribers through targeted email campaigns and incentives.

d. Promotions and Sales: Promote products, offer discounts, and drive sales through well-timed email campaigns.

e. Personalization: Tailor email content and offers based on customer preferences and behavior.

f. Automation: Automation tools streamline repetitive tasks, such as sending welcome emails, abandoned cart reminders, and order confirmations.

2. Email Marketing Strategies

Here are key strategies for leveraging email marketing as your dropshipping business scales:

a. Build an Email List: Encourage website visitors to subscribe to your email list through sign-up forms, incentives like discounts, or newsletters.

b. Segment Your List: Divide your email list into segments based on customer behavior, demographics, or purchase history. Send targeted campaigns to each segment.

c. Create Engaging Content: Craft compelling email content, including product recommendations, promotional offers, and valuable information.

d. Automate Workflows: Set up automation workflows for tasks like welcoming new subscribers, recovering abandoned carts, and post-purchase follow-ups.

e. Monitor and Analyze: Regularly review email analytics to assess the performance of your campaigns. Adjust your strategies based on what works best.

3. Email Marketing Tools

Consider utilizing the following email marketing tools to enhance your dropshipping business:

a. Mailchimp: Mailchimp is a user-friendly email marketing platform that offers automation features, customizable templates, and detailed analytics.

b. Klaviyo: Klaviyo is designed for e-commerce businesses and specializes in email automation, segmentation, and personalized messaging.

c. ConvertKit: ConvertKit is a robust email marketing tool that caters to bloggers, content creators, and small businesses. It offers advanced automation and segmentation capabilities.

d. Omnisend: Omnisend is an omnichannel marketing automation platform that specializes in email and SMS marketing for e-commerce. It includes automation workflows and audience segmentation.

e. ActiveCampaign: ActiveCampaign is an all-in-one marketing automation platform that combines email marketing with CRM features, making it suitable for advanced automation and customer relationship management.

f. Drip: Drip is an e-commerce CRM and marketing automation platform that focuses on personalization and customer journey automation.

4. Implementing Email Marketing Strategies

To make the most of email marketing:

a. Build an Email List: Encourage website visitors to subscribe to your email list through sign-up forms and incentives like discounts or newsletters.

b. Segment Your List: Divide your email list into segments based on customer behavior, demographics, or purchase history. Send targeted campaigns to each segment.

c. Create Engaging Content: Craft compelling email content, including product recommendations, promotional offers, and valuable information.

d. Automate Workflows: Set up automation workflows for tasks like welcoming new subscribers, recovering abandoned carts, and post-purchase follow-ups.

e. Monitor and Analyze: Regularly review email analytics to assess the performance of your campaigns. Adjust your strategies based on what works best.

Email marketing is a versatile and effective tool for maintaining customer engagement, driving sales, and building brand loyalty as your dropshipping business scales. By harnessing the power of email marketing and implementing best practices, you can stay connected with your audience and nurture long-term customer relationships. In the following sections, we'll explore additional methods to enhance your online presence, expand your marketing efforts, and scale your dropshipping venture further.

Chapter 5: Establishing a Strong Brand Presence

5.4 Using Paid Advertising Effectively

Paid advertising is a dynamic and strategic way to expand your dropshipping business's reach, attract potential customers, and boost sales. As your business scales, employing paid advertising effectively becomes essential to maximize your marketing efforts. In this section, we will explore the significance of paid advertising and provide strategies to make the most of it for your brand.

1. The Power of Paid Advertising

Paid advertising offers a range of advantages for your dropshipping business:

a. Targeted Reach: Paid ads allow you to reach specific demographics, interests, and behaviors, ensuring that your message reaches the right audience.

b. Quick Visibility: Unlike organic methods, paid advertising can generate immediate visibility and traffic to your online store.

c. Scalability: You can control the budget and scale of your advertising campaigns, making it adaptable to your business growth.

d. Measurable Results: Paid advertising platforms provide detailed analytics, allowing you to measure the effectiveness of your campaigns and make data-driven decisions.

2. Strategies for Using Paid Advertising Effectively

Here are key strategies for using paid advertising effectively as your dropshipping business scales:

a. Platform Selection: Choose the right advertising platforms based on your target audience and objectives. Common platforms include Google Ads, Facebook Ads, Instagram Ads, Pinterest Ads, and more.

b. Audience Targeting: Define your target audience precisely by demographics, interests, behaviors, and location to ensure your ads reach the most relevant potential customers.

c. Keyword Research: For search engine advertising (e.g., Google Ads), conduct thorough keyword research to identify high-converting keywords that align with your products.

d. Compelling Ad Copy: Craft compelling and concise ad copy that highlights the benefits of your products and encourages clicks.

e. Visual Appeal: Design eye-catching ad creatives, including images and videos, that resonate with your target audience and align with your brand.

f. A/B Testing: Continually test different ad variations to optimize ad performance. Experiment with headlines, ad copy, visuals, and calls to action.

g. Landing Pages: Ensure that the landing pages your ads direct users to are relevant, well-designed, and optimized for conversions.

h. Budget Management: Set a clear budget for your advertising campaigns and monitor spending to stay within your limits.

i. Conversion Tracking: Implement conversion tracking to measure the impact of your ads on sales and other key performance indicators (KPIs).

j. Remarketing: Use remarketing campaigns to target users who have previously interacted with your website or products but did not make a purchase.

k. Ad Scheduling: Schedule your ads to run during peak hours or when your target audience is most active online.

l. Monitoring and Optimization: Regularly monitor your ad campaigns, analyze performance metrics, and make adjustments to improve ROI.

3. Paid Advertising Platforms

Explore various paid advertising platforms to determine which aligns best with your goals:

a. Google Ads: Ideal for search and display advertising, reaching users actively searching for products or services.

b. Facebook Ads: Offers a wide range of ad formats and audience targeting options, suitable for both B2B and B2C businesses.

c. Instagram Ads: Ideal for visually appealing products and brands targeting a younger demographic.

d. Pinterest Ads: Effective for e-commerce businesses with visually appealing products and a female-centric audience.

e. Twitter Ads: Suited for brands looking to promote content, events, and news updates.

f. LinkedIn Ads: Targeted towards B2B businesses and professionals looking to reach specific industries and job roles.

g. TikTok Ads: Ideal for businesses targeting a younger, trend-conscious audience with video content.

4. Performance Monitoring

Consistently monitor and analyze the performance of your paid advertising campaigns. Adjust your strategies based on insights gained from ad analytics to optimize your ROI.

Paid advertising is a powerful tool that can significantly impact your dropshipping business's growth and profitability. By employing effective paid advertising strategies and platforms, you can expand your reach, attract qualified leads, and drive conversions. In the following sections, we'll explore additional methods to enhance your online presence, expand your marketing efforts, and scale your dropshipping venture further.

Chapter 6: Scaling Your Dropshipping Business

Welcome to the sixth and final chapter of "Maximizing Profits with WooCommerce: The Ultimate Guide to Dropshipping from AliExpress." You've come a long way in your dropshipping journey, from setting up your online store to mastering its operations and marketing. Now, it's time to explore one of the most exciting aspects of entrepreneurship: scaling your business for growth and profitability.

Scaling your dropshipping business involves expanding its reach, increasing sales, and optimizing your operations to accommodate higher demand. Whether you're just starting to think about scaling or you're already experiencing growth, this chapter will provide you with valuable insights and strategies to help you take your business to the next level.

Here's what you can expect to explore in this chapter:

1. Product Expansion: Learn how to diversify your product offerings to attract a broader audience and increase your revenue streams. We'll discuss sourcing from additional suppliers, exploring new product categories, and staying on top of market trends.

2. Market Expansion: Explore strategies for entering new markets, both domestically and internationally. We'll cover market research, localization, and adapting your marketing efforts to target different regions.

3. Inventory Management: Discover advanced inventory management techniques to handle larger product catalogs and higher sales volumes. We'll discuss strategies for efficient stock management, backorders, and avoiding overstock situations.

4. Order Fulfillment Optimization: Fine-tune your order processing and fulfillment operations to accommodate increased orders seamlessly. Learn about automating order workflows and optimizing supplier relationships.

5. Customer Retention: Explore strategies for retaining existing customers and turning them into repeat buyers. Loyal customers are an invaluable asset to your business.

6. Marketing at Scale: Refine your marketing strategies to reach a broader audience and maximize your marketing budget. We'll discuss scaling your advertising efforts, expanding your content marketing, and using data-driven insights to drive growth.

7. Operational Efficiency: Implement processes and systems that improve the efficiency of your dropshipping operations. As your business grows, optimizing processes becomes crucial to maintaining profitability.

8. Financial Management: Learn how to manage your finances effectively as your business scales. We'll discuss budgeting, cash flow management, and financial forecasting.

Throughout this chapter, we'll provide practical advice, best practices, and real-world examples to help you navigate the challenges and opportunities of scaling your dropshipping business. Whether you're looking to double your sales or expand internationally, the insights you gain here will be instrumental in achieving your growth objectives.

By the end of this chapter, you'll be well-equipped to scale your dropshipping business with confidence, making informed decisions that lead to sustained success and profitability. So, let's embark on this final stage of your journey, where the sky's the limit for your dropshipping venture. Let's get started!

6.1 Expanding Your Product Range

As your dropshipping business grows, one of the key strategies to explore is expanding your product range. Offering a diverse selection of products can attract a broader customer base, increase order values, and contribute to long-term success. In this section, we will delve into the importance of product range expansion and provide strategies to effectively introduce new products to your store.

1. The Significance of Product Range Expansion

Expanding your product range offers several benefits for your dropshipping business:

a. Attracting a Wider Audience: A broader product range can appeal to a wider range of customers with varying preferences and needs.

b. Increasing Sales Opportunities: By offering more products, you create additional opportunities for customers to make purchases, potentially leading to higher order values.

c. Diversifying Revenue Streams: A diverse product range can help you mitigate the impact of seasonality or market fluctuations by relying on multiple revenue streams.

d. Cross-Selling and Upselling: Additional products can facilitate cross-selling and upselling, encouraging customers to explore and purchase related items.

e. Competitive Advantage: A comprehensive product range can give you an edge over competitors who offer a limited selection.

2. Strategies for Expanding Your Product Range

Here are key strategies to effectively expand your product range as your dropshipping business scales:

a. Market Research: Conduct thorough market research to identify product categories or niches that align with your brand and have strong demand.

b. Supplier Evaluation: Collaborate with reliable suppliers who can consistently provide quality products and ensure reliable shipping.

c. Complementary Products: Consider adding complementary or related products to your existing offerings. For example, if you sell fitness equipment, expand to include workout apparel and accessories.

d. Trend Analysis: Keep an eye on industry trends and customer preferences to identify emerging product categories or seasonal opportunities.

e. Test New Products: Introduce new products gradually and assess their performance. Pay attention to customer feedback and sales data to refine your offerings.

f. Product Listings: Optimize product listings with detailed descriptions, high-quality images, and clear pricing to attract potential buyers.

g. Inventory Management: Implement efficient inventory management practices to ensure accurate stock levels and minimize the risk of overselling.

h. Marketing and Promotion: Create targeted marketing campaigns to introduce new products to your audience. Use email marketing, social media, and paid advertising to generate interest.

i. Customer Feedback: Encourage customers to provide feedback and reviews for new products, building trust and credibility.

j. Seasonal Offerings: Offer seasonal or holiday-themed products to capitalize on festive shopping trends.

k. Competitive Pricing: Strategically price new products to remain competitive while maintaining profitability.

l. Cross-Sell and Upsell: Implement cross-selling and upselling techniques to encourage customers to explore and purchase additional products.

3. Product Quality and Reliability

Maintaining product quality and reliability is crucial when expanding your product range. Ensure that new products meet the same standards as your existing offerings to maintain customer trust.

4. Supplier Relationships

Nurture strong relationships with your suppliers to secure consistent access to products and reliable shipping. Communication and collaboration are key.

5. Inventory Management

Implement robust inventory management practices, including real-time tracking and automated restocking, to effectively handle a larger product range.

6. Customer Education

Educate your customers about new product offerings through informative content, tutorials, and guides to encourage adoption.

Expanding your product range can breathe new life into your dropshipping business and open doors to untapped markets and opportunities. By carefully selecting products, optimizing your listings, and effectively marketing your expanded offerings, you can enhance your brand's appeal and drive growth. In the following sections, we'll explore additional strategies for scaling your dropshipping venture, enhancing customer engagement, and maximizing profitability.

6.2 Optimizing for Higher Conversion Rates

Conversion rate optimization (CRO) is a critical aspect of scaling your dropshipping business. It involves improving your website and marketing efforts to encourage more visitors to take desired actions, such as making a purchase or subscribing to your email list. In this section, we will delve into the significance of conversion rate optimization and provide strategies to boost your website's performance and drive higher conversion rates.

1. The Importance of Conversion Rate Optimization

Conversion rate optimization is essential for several reasons:

a. Increased Revenue: A higher conversion rate means more customers are taking action, which directly translates to increased revenue.

b. Cost Efficiency: CRO allows you to make the most of your existing traffic, reducing the need to spend more on acquiring new visitors.

c. Improved User Experience: Optimizing your website enhances the user experience, leading to higher customer satisfaction and loyalty.

d. Competitive Advantage: A well-optimized website can set you apart from competitors and attract more customers in a crowded market.

e. Data-Driven Decisions: CRO relies on data analysis, allowing you to make informed decisions based on customer behavior and preferences.

2. Strategies for Higher Conversion Rates

Here are key strategies to optimize for higher conversion rates as your dropshipping business scales:

a. A/B Testing: Conduct A/B tests to compare different versions of web pages, product listings, and marketing materials to determine what resonates best with your audience.

b. User-Friendly Design: Ensure your website is easy to navigate and mobile-responsive. Simplify the checkout process and reduce friction to encourage conversions.

c. Compelling Content: Craft persuasive product descriptions, captivating headlines, and engaging visuals to convey the value of your products.

d. Social Proof: Showcase customer reviews, testimonials, and trust badges to build credibility and trust.

e. Call-to-Action (CTA): Use clear and prominent CTAs that guide visitors towards the desired actions, such as "Add to Cart" or "Buy Now."

f. Trust Signals: Display trust signals like secure payment icons, return policies, and contact information to reassure customers.

g. Personalization: Implement personalized recommendations based on user behavior and preferences to encourage relevant product exploration.

h. Loading Speed: Optimize website loading speed to prevent visitors from abandoning your site due to slow performance.

i. Exit-Intent Popups: Use exit-intent popups to capture potential leads or offer special discounts to visitors who are about to leave your site.

j. Customer Support: Provide easy access to customer support options, such as live chat, email, or a contact form, to address any questions or concerns promptly.

k. Abandoned Cart Recovery: Implement automated abandoned cart recovery emails to encourage customers to complete their purchase.

l. Detailed Product Information: Offer comprehensive product information, including specifications, sizing charts, and FAQs, to address common customer queries.

3. Analytics and Tracking

Use web analytics tools like Google Analytics to track user behavior, conversion funnels, and identify areas where improvements are needed.

4. Customer Feedback

Gather feedback from customers to gain insights into their experience and identify pain points that may be hindering conversions.

5. Continuous Improvement

CRO is an ongoing process. Continuously analyze data, test new ideas, and make iterative improvements to your website and marketing strategies.

6. Performance Monitoring

Regularly monitor and analyze the performance of your optimization efforts to measure their impact on conversion rates and adjust as needed.

Optimizing for higher conversion rates is a dynamic process that can significantly impact your dropshipping business's success and profitability. By implementing these strategies and staying attuned to customer preferences and behavior, you can create a more compelling and effective online shopping experience. In the following sections, we'll explore additional strategies for enhancing your online presence, expanding your marketing efforts, and scaling your dropshipping venture further.

6.3 Collaborating with Influencers and Affiliates

In the digital age, harnessing the power of influencers and affiliates can be a game-changer for your dropshipping business's growth. These collaborations allow you to tap into established audiences and build trust with potential customers. In this section, we will explore the significance of influencer and affiliate marketing and provide strategies to effectively collaborate with them.

1. The Influence of Influencers and Affiliates

Influencers and affiliates play a vital role in modern marketing for several reasons:

a. Audience Trust: Influencers have built trust with their followers, and their endorsements can carry significant weight.

b. Expanded Reach: Collaborating with influencers and affiliates exposes your brand to their established and engaged audiences.

c. Cost-Effective Marketing: Affiliate marketing often involves paying for performance, ensuring a return on investment (ROI).

d. Diverse Promotion: Different influencers and affiliates cater to various niches and demographics, allowing you to diversify your marketing efforts.

e. Authenticity: Influencers and affiliates can provide authentic and relatable content that resonates with their audiences.

2. Strategies for Collaborating with Influencers and Affiliates

Here are key strategies to effectively collaborate with influencers and affiliates as your dropshipping business scales:

a. Identify Relevant Partners: Research and identify influencers and affiliates whose audiences align with your target market and products.

b. Establish Clear Terms: Define clear terms of collaboration, including compensation, content guidelines, and performance metrics.

c. Quality Over Quantity: Focus on building relationships with a select few influencers or affiliates who have a genuine connection with your brand.

d. Authentic Content: Encourage influencers and affiliates to create authentic content that showcases your products in a relatable manner.

e. Monitor Performance: Track the performance of influencer and affiliate campaigns, measuring metrics like click-through rates, conversions, and ROI.

f. Provide Resources: Offer influencers and affiliates the resources they need, such as product samples, promotional materials, and tracking links.

g. Compliance and Disclosure: Ensure that influencer and affiliate partnerships comply with relevant advertising regulations and include proper disclosure.

h. Long-Term Relationships: Nurture long-term relationships with influencers and affiliates who consistently deliver results and align with your brand values.

i. Affiliate Programs: Implement an affiliate program with a user-friendly platform that allows affiliates to easily access promotional materials and track their earnings.

j. Diversify Partnerships: Collaborate with influencers and affiliates from various niches and platforms to reach a diverse audience.

3. Due Diligence

Before collaborating with influencers and affiliates, conduct due diligence to vet their authenticity, engagement rates, and alignment with your brand values.

4. Contractual Agreements

Create formal contractual agreements outlining the terms of collaboration, payment structures, and performance expectations.

5. Performance Tracking

Utilize tracking tools and analytics to monitor the performance of influencer and affiliate marketing efforts and adjust strategies as needed.

6. Feedback and Improvement

Seek feedback from influencers, affiliates, and customers to continually improve your collaboration strategies and offerings.

Collaborating with influencers and affiliates can be a powerful way to reach new audiences, build brand credibility, and drive conversions. By strategically selecting partners, setting clear terms, and nurturing long-term relationships, you can effectively leverage the influence of these marketing channels. In the following sections, we'll explore additional strategies for enhancing your online presence, expanding your marketing efforts, and scaling your dropshipping venture further.

6.4 Exploring International Markets

Expanding your dropshipping business to international markets can open up a world of opportunities for growth and increased revenue. As your business scales, considering international expansion becomes a strategic move to reach a global audience. In this section, we will explore the significance of tapping into international markets and provide strategies to effectively expand your presence beyond borders.

1. The Global Opportunity

Expanding into international markets offers several compelling advantages:

a. Diversified Customer Base: Accessing international markets diversifies your customer base, reducing dependence on a single market.

b. Increased Revenue: International expansion can significantly increase your revenue potential by tapping into larger and emerging markets.

c. Competitive Edge: Entering new markets can give you a competitive edge over rivals who have not ventured beyond their domestic market.

d. Seasonal Balancing: International markets can help balance seasonal fluctuations in demand, ensuring year-round sales.

e. Brand Exposure: Expanding globally can enhance your brand's reputation and visibility on a global scale.

2. Strategies for International Expansion

Here are key strategies to effectively explore and expand into international markets:

a. Market Research: Conduct thorough market research to identify target countries with demand for your products and assess market viability.

b. Localized Marketing: Adapt your marketing strategies to cater to the cultural, linguistic, and behavioral differences of each international market.

c. Currency and Pricing: Adjust product pricing and currency options to accommodate the preferences and purchasing power of international customers.

d. Shipping and Logistics: Establish reliable shipping and logistics solutions to ensure timely and cost-effective international deliveries.

e. Multilingual Customer Support: Offer multilingual customer support to address inquiries and concerns from international customers.

f. Compliance and Regulations: Familiarize yourself with international trade regulations, customs requirements, and tax implications for each market.

g. Payment Options: Provide a variety of payment options that cater to the preferences of international customers.

h. Localization: Localize your website, including language, currency, and product descriptions, to create a user-friendly experience.

i. Partner with Local Influencers: Collaborate with local influencers in target markets to enhance your brand's reach and credibility.

j. Competitive Analysis: Analyze the competition in international markets and identify strategies to differentiate your offerings.

k. Testing and Adaptation: Start with a soft launch or pilot in select international markets to test the waters before full-scale expansion.

l. Cross-Border Returns: Plan for cross-border returns and establish clear return policies for international customers.

3. Risk Assessment

Assess potential risks associated with international expansion, such as currency fluctuations, regulatory challenges, and cultural differences, and develop mitigation strategies.

4. Localization

Invest in localization efforts to ensure that your website, marketing materials, and customer support are tailored to the specific needs of each international market.

5. Local Partnerships

Consider partnering with local distributors, fulfillment centers, or suppliers to streamline operations and provide a better customer experience.

6. Performance Monitoring

Regularly monitor the performance of your international expansion efforts, including sales, customer feedback, and market trends, and make adjustments accordingly.

Exploring international markets is a strategic step toward scaling your dropshipping business and unlocking new growth opportunities. By carefully researching and planning for international expansion, adapting to local preferences, and providing exceptional customer experiences, you can successfully tap into global markets. In the following sections, we'll explore additional strategies for enhancing your online presence, expanding your marketing efforts, and optimizing your dropshipping venture for continued success.

Chapter 7: Legal and Financial Considerations

Congratulations on reaching Chapter 7 of "Maximizing Profits with WooCommerce: The Ultimate Guide to Dropshipping from AliExpress." As you've navigated through the various facets of building and growing your dropshipping business, it's important not to overlook the critical aspects of legality and finance. In this chapter, we'll dive into the essential legal and financial considerations every dropshipper should be aware of.

Running a dropshipping business successfully requires more than just finding great products and marketing effectively; it also involves adhering to legal regulations and managing your finances prudently. Neglecting these aspects can lead to costly mistakes and potential legal issues down the road. Therefore, it's crucial to understand and address these matters proactively.

Here's what you can expect to explore in this chapter:

1. Business Structure: Learn about different business structures (e.g., sole proprietorship, LLC, corporation) and how to choose the one that best suits your dropshipping business. Your choice affects liability, taxes, and more.

2. Legal Compliance: Understand the legal requirements and regulations that apply to your e-commerce business, including business licenses, permits, and tax obligations.

3. Intellectual Property: Explore the nuances of intellectual property laws, including trademarks, copyrights, and patents. Understand how to protect your own intellectual property and respect the rights of others.

4. Privacy and Data Protection: Learn about data protection laws and regulations (such as GDPR) and how they apply to your dropshipping store, especially if you collect customer data.

5. Taxes: Gain insights into tax considerations for your dropshipping business, including sales tax, income tax, and international tax implications. We'll discuss how to handle tax collection and reporting.

6. Financial Management: Explore advanced financial management techniques for your business, including budgeting, financial forecasting, and optimizing cash flow.

7. Insurance: Understand the importance of insurance for your dropshipping business, including liability insurance and coverage for potential risks and losses.

8. Legal Agreements: Discover the key legal agreements and documents you should have in place, such as terms and conditions, privacy policies, and supplier agreements.

9. Dispute Resolution: Learn how to handle disputes and conflicts with customers or suppliers, including strategies for resolving issues amicably.

Throughout this chapter, we'll provide practical guidance, highlight common pitfalls to avoid, and offer resources to help you navigate the legal and financial landscape of your dropshipping business effectively. Whether you're just starting out or looking to ensure your existing business is on solid legal and financial footing, the insights you gain here will be invaluable.

By the end of this chapter, you'll have a clear understanding of the legal and financial considerations associated with dropshipping, and you'll be better prepared to manage these aspects as your business continues to grow. So, let's dive into the world of legal and financial matters, ensuring that your dropshipping venture remains compliant, secure, and financially sound. Let's get started!

7.1 Understanding Dropshipping Legalities

Operating a dropshipping business can be rewarding, but it also comes with legal responsibilities and considerations that are essential to understand and adhere to. In this section, we will explore the various legal aspects of dropshipping, ensuring that you are well-informed about the legal requirements and best practices that apply to your business.

1. The Legal Landscape

Dropshipping, like any business model, operates within a legal framework that includes various laws and regulations. Understanding and complying with these legalities is crucial to protect your business and ensure its long-term viability. Key legal aspects to consider include:

a. Business Registration: Depending on your location and the scale of your business, you may need to register your dropshipping business as a legal entity, such as a sole proprietorship, LLC, or corporation.

b. Sales Tax: Sales tax regulations vary by location and are subject to change. It's essential to be aware of your obligations regarding the collection and remittance of sales tax.

c. Import and Export Laws: If you're dropshipping internationally, you'll need to comply with import and export laws, including customs regulations and tariffs.

d. Intellectual Property: Respect intellectual property rights, including trademarks, copyrights, and patents. Avoid selling counterfeit or infringing products.

e. Privacy and Data Protection: Safeguard customer data and comply with data protection laws, such as GDPR (General Data Protection Regulation) in the European Union.

f. Advertising and Marketing: Adhere to advertising standards, avoid false claims, and comply with regulations related to email marketing and online advertising.

g. Consumer Protection: Understand consumer protection laws that govern product warranties, returns, and refunds.

h. Contracts and Agreements: Establish clear and legally binding contracts with suppliers, partners, affiliates, and influencers.

i. Website Policies: Create and display essential policies on your website, including terms of service, privacy policy, and return policy.

2. Compliance and Due Diligence

Compliance with legal requirements and due diligence in your business operations are essential. This involves:

a. Research: Continuously research and stay updated on relevant laws and regulations in your industry and target markets.

b. Consultation: Seek legal advice or consultation if needed to ensure that your business practices align with the law.

c. Documentation: Maintain accurate records of all business transactions, contracts, and legal documents.

d. Transparency: Be transparent with customers regarding your business practices, policies, and product information.

e. Customer Protection: Prioritize customer satisfaction and promptly address any legal issues or disputes.

f. Ethical Conduct: Uphold ethical business conduct and avoid engaging in deceptive or fraudulent activities.

g. Ongoing Monitoring: Regularly review and adapt your business practices to remain in compliance with evolving legal requirements.

3. International Considerations

If you operate internationally or plan to expand into global markets, be aware that different countries may have distinct legal requirements and regulations. Conduct thorough research and adapt your business practices accordingly to ensure compliance in each jurisdiction you serve.

4. Legal Resources

Explore legal resources and consider consulting legal professionals who specialize in e-commerce and dropshipping to guide you in navigating the legal complexities of your business.

Understanding dropshipping legalities is crucial for the success and sustainability of your business. By proactively addressing legal considerations, adhering to regulations, and maintaining ethical business conduct, you can mitigate legal risks and build a reputable dropshipping venture. In the following sections, we'll delve deeper into specific legal aspects and provide guidance on how to navigate them effectively.

Certainly, here's an introduction for section 7.2 of your guide titled "Tax Implications and Compliance":

7.2 Tax Implications and Compliance

Navigating the tax landscape is a crucial aspect of running a successful dropshipping business. Understanding the tax implications and ensuring compliance with tax regulations is essential to avoid legal issues and financial penalties. In this section, we will delve into the tax considerations that apply to dropshipping and provide strategies for tax compliance.

1. Taxation in Dropshipping

Taxation in dropshipping involves various aspects that require attention:

a. Sales Tax: Depending on your location and the locations where you have economic nexus (a significant presence), you may be required to collect and remit sales tax on sales to customers.

b. Value Added Tax (VAT): If you operate internationally or sell to customers in countries that impose VAT, you need to understand and comply with VAT requirements.

c. Income Tax: As a business owner, you are subject to income tax on the profits generated by your dropshipping business.

d. Import Duties and Customs Fees: International dropshipping may involve import duties and customs fees imposed by the destination country, which you or your customers may be responsible for.

e. Withholding Tax: If you collaborate with affiliates, influencers, or partners from different countries, you may be subject to withholding tax on payments made to them.

2. Strategies for Tax Compliance

To ensure tax compliance in your dropshipping business, consider the following strategies:

a. Registration: Determine whether you need to register for sales tax, VAT, or any other relevant taxes based on your business location and customer base.

b. Collection and Remittance: Collect the appropriate taxes from customers during the checkout process and remit them to the relevant tax authorities on time.

c. Accounting Software: Utilize accounting software or hire a professional accountant to keep accurate records of your business transactions and tax obligations.

d. International Tax Expertise: If you operate internationally, seek the expertise of international tax professionals who can help you navigate the complexities of cross-border taxation.

e. Compliance Software: Consider using tax compliance software that can automatically calculate and collect taxes for you based on the customer's location.

f. Regular Reporting: File tax returns and reports accurately and punctually to avoid penalties and legal issues.

g. Stay Informed: Continuously educate yourself about changes in tax laws and regulations that may affect your dropshipping business.

h. Consultation: When in doubt, consult with a tax attorney or accountant who specializes in e-commerce and dropshipping to ensure full compliance.

3. State and International Tax Considerations

Be aware that tax regulations can vary significantly from one state or country to another. Ensure you understand the specific tax requirements in the jurisdictions where you operate or sell your products.

4. Record Keeping

Maintain comprehensive records of your business transactions, including sales, expenses, and tax-related documents. These records are vital for tax audits and reporting.

5. Audits and Penalties

Failure to comply with tax regulations can lead to audits and substantial penalties. It's crucial to prioritize tax compliance to protect your business.

Navigating tax implications and ensuring compliance is a fundamental aspect of managing a dropshipping business. By proactively addressing tax considerations, staying informed about changes in tax laws, and seeking professional guidance when needed, you can protect your business from legal issues and financial setbacks. In the following sections, we'll explore additional legal and operational aspects to help you run a successful and compliant dropshipping venture.

7.3 Setting Up Business Finances

Effective financial management is at the core of any successful dropshipping business. To maintain financial stability, make informed decisions, and ensure compliance with tax and legal obligations, setting up and managing your business finances is essential. In this section, we will delve into the key aspects of establishing and maintaining sound financial practices for your dropshipping venture.

1. The Importance of Sound Financial Practices

Sound financial practices are the foundation of a thriving dropshipping business for several reasons:

a. Financial Control: Maintaining control over your finances allows you to make informed decisions and allocate resources strategically.

b. Tax Compliance: Proper financial management ensures that you can meet tax obligations accurately and on time, reducing the risk of penalties.

c. Growth and Expansion: Effective financial planning and budgeting enable you to fund business growth and explore new opportunities.

d. Risk Mitigation: A well-structured financial strategy can help you navigate economic challenges and unexpected expenses.

e. Investor Confidence: If you plan to seek investors or loans, organized finances instill confidence in potential stakeholders.

2. Strategies for Setting Up Business Finances

Here are key strategies to set up and manage your dropshipping business finances effectively:

a. Separate Business and Personal Finances: Open a dedicated business bank account to keep personal and business finances separate, simplifying accounting and tax compliance.

b. Accounting Software: Utilize accounting software to track income, expenses, and sales tax accurately. Popular options include QuickBooks, Xero, and Wave.

c. Budgeting: Create a budget that outlines your expected revenue, expenses, and profit margins. Regularly review and adjust the budget as needed.

d. Record Keeping: Maintain meticulous records of all financial transactions, including sales receipts, supplier invoices, and tax documents.

e. Tax Planning: Plan for tax payments and set aside a portion of your income to cover tax obligations. Consult with a tax professional for guidance.

f. Financial Reports: Generate and analyze financial reports, such as profit and loss statements and cash flow statements, to assess your business's financial health.

g. Payment Processing: Choose reliable payment processors and ensure secure and efficient payment processing for customer orders.

h. Supplier Payments: Establish clear payment terms with your suppliers and adhere to payment schedules to maintain good working relationships.

i. Debt Management: If you have loans or credit lines, manage them responsibly to avoid excessive interest and debt burdens.

j. Reserve Fund: Create an emergency fund or reserve to cover unexpected expenses or revenue fluctuations.

k. Profit Reinvestment: Reinvest a portion of your profits back into your business for growth and expansion.

l. Financial Advisors: Consider consulting financial advisors or accountants who specialize in e-commerce to receive expert guidance.

3. Financial Analysis

Regularly analyze your financial data to identify trends, areas of improvement, and opportunities for cost-saving or revenue enhancement.

4. Tax Preparation

Prepare for tax season well in advance by maintaining accurate financial records and consulting with a tax professional to ensure compliance.

5. Financial Growth Strategies

Explore strategies to increase your business's profitability, such as optimizing pricing, reducing expenses, and diversifying product offerings.

Effective financial management is a fundamental component of building a successful and sustainable dropshipping business. By implementing sound financial practices, monitoring your finances regularly, and seeking expert guidance when needed, you can establish a strong financial foundation that supports your business's growth and stability. In the following sections, we'll explore additional legal and operational aspects to help you run a compliant and thriving dropshipping venture.

7.4 Protecting Your Business with Insurances

Running a dropshipping business comes with inherent risks, and unforeseen events can have a significant impact on your operations and financial stability. To safeguard your business from potential liabilities and losses, it's crucial to consider insurance coverage tailored to your specific needs. In this section, we will explore the importance of business insurance and provide guidance on protecting your dropshipping venture.

1. The Significance of Business Insurance

Business insurance plays a vital role in protecting your dropshipping business for various reasons:

a. Risk Mitigation: Insurance coverage helps mitigate financial risks associated with unforeseen events, such as product liability claims, theft, or damage to inventory.

b. Legal Requirements: Depending on your location and the nature of your business, certain types of insurance, such as workers' compensation or general liability insurance, may be legally required.

c. Peace of Mind: Knowing that you are adequately insured provides peace of mind and allows you to focus on growing your business without constant worry about potential losses.

d. Financial Resilience: Insurance can provide financial support to help your business recover from setbacks, such as natural disasters or legal disputes.

e. Vendor Requirements: Some suppliers and e-commerce platforms may require proof of insurance as a condition of doing business with them.

2. Types of Business Insurance

There are several types of business insurance to consider for your dropshipping venture, including:

a. General Liability Insurance: Protects your business from claims related to bodily injury, property damage, or advertising injury.

b. Product Liability Insurance: Specifically covers claims related to product defects or injuries caused by the products you sell.

c. Property Insurance: Covers damage to your business property, including inventory, due to events like fire, theft, or natural disasters.

d. Cyber Liability Insurance: Helps protect against data breaches and cyberattacks, which can compromise customer data and reputation.

e. Business Interruption Insurance: Provides financial support in case your business operations are disrupted due to unforeseen events, allowing you to recover lost income.

f. Workers' Compensation Insurance: If you have employees, this insurance is typically required and covers medical expenses and lost wages in case of work-related injuries.

g. Cargo Insurance: If you handle shipping and logistics, cargo insurance can protect your inventory during transit.

h. Professional Liability Insurance: Also known as errors and omissions insurance, this coverage is relevant if you offer professional advice or services.

3. Assessing Insurance Needs

Determine your specific insurance needs by considering factors such as the nature of your products, business location, revenue, and potential risks. Consulting with an insurance professional can help you tailor coverage to your unique situation.

4. Insurance Providers

Research and compare insurance providers to find policies that offer the coverage you need at competitive rates. Consider reaching out to insurance brokers or agents who specialize in e-commerce and small businesses.

5. Policy Review

Regularly review your insurance policies to ensure they align with your evolving business needs and to make any necessary adjustments.

6. Documentation

Keep records of your insurance policies, premiums, and payment receipts in a secure location for easy access in case of claims.

Protecting your dropshipping business with the right insurance coverage is a crucial step in ensuring its long-term viability and resilience against unforeseen events. By assessing your insurance needs, selecting appropriate coverage, and staying informed about your policy terms and conditions, you can mitigate potential risks and focus on growing your business with confidence. In the following sections, we'll explore additional legal and operational aspects to help you run a compliant and thriving dropshipping venture.

Chapter 8: Advanced Dropshipping Strategies

Welcome to the final chapter of "Maximizing Profits with WooCommerce: The Ultimate Guide to Dropshipping from AliExpress." By now, you've journeyed through the essential elements of setting up, running, and growing a successful dropshipping business. In this concluding chapter, we'll explore advanced dropshipping strategies that can elevate your business to new heights of profitability and sustainability.

As an experienced dropshipper or a determined entrepreneur, you understand that the e-commerce landscape is dynamic and ever-evolving. Staying ahead of the competition requires innovation, adaptation, and a deep understanding of your market and customers. The strategies outlined in this chapter are designed to help you do just that.

Here's a glimpse of what you can expect to explore in this chapter:

1. Multi-Supplier Sourcing: Diversify your supplier base and reduce risk by sourcing products from multiple AliExpress suppliers. We'll discuss strategies for managing multiple suppliers efficiently.

2. Branding and Private Labeling: Learn how to build a strong brand identity and consider private labeling products to stand out in a crowded market and command higher prices.

3. Customized Packaging: Discover the impact of customized packaging on customer experience and brand perception. We'll explore options for creating unique, branded packaging for your products.

4. International Expansion: Explore strategies for expanding your dropshipping business internationally, tapping into new markets, and leveraging global opportunities.

5. Subscription Box Model: Consider implementing a subscription box model to increase customer retention, build recurring revenue, and create a loyal customer base.

6. Cross-Selling and Upselling: Learn how to effectively cross-sell and upsell products to maximize the value of each customer transaction.

7. Marketplace Diversification: Explore the potential of selling on multiple online marketplaces, such

as Amazon, eBay, or Etsy, in addition to your WooCommerce store.

8. Advanced Marketing Tactics: Dive into advanced marketing strategies, including influencer partnerships, affiliate marketing, and data-driven marketing techniques.

9. Customer Retention and Loyalty: Implement strategies to foster long-term customer relationships, increase customer lifetime value, and reduce churn.

Throughout this chapter, we'll provide in-depth insights, real-world examples, and actionable steps to help you implement these advanced dropshipping strategies effectively. Whether you're aiming for rapid growth, brand differentiation, or exploring new revenue streams, the knowledge and techniques you acquire here will be instrumental in achieving your goals.

By the end of this chapter, you'll be equipped with the tools and strategies to propel your dropshipping business into the advanced stages of success. So, let's dive into the world of advanced dropshipping strategies, where innovation and expertise combine to take your business to new heights. Let's get started!

8.1 Utilizing Data for Business Decisions

In the dynamic landscape of e-commerce and dropshipping, data is a valuable asset that can empower you to make informed and strategic business decisions. By harnessing the power of data, you can gain deeper insights into customer behavior, market trends, and the performance of your dropshipping venture. In this section, we will explore the significance of data-driven decision making and provide strategies for leveraging data effectively.

1. The Role of Data in Dropshipping

Data serves as the foundation for informed decision making in your dropshipping business for several reasons:

a. Customer Insights: Data helps you understand your customers' preferences, buying habits, and demographics, allowing you to tailor your offerings and marketing efforts.

b. Inventory Management: Data-driven forecasting and analysis enable efficient inventory management, reducing the risk of overstocking or stockouts.

c. Pricing Strategies: Data can inform your pricing strategies by evaluating competitive pricing, demand elasticity, and profitability.

d. Marketing Effectiveness: Analyzing data helps you measure the ROI of marketing campaigns, enabling you to allocate resources to the most effective channels.

e. Trend Identification: Data allows you to identify market trends, emerging product categories, and seasonal demand shifts.

f. Performance Evaluation: Data-driven KPIs (Key Performance Indicators) help you assess the performance of your business and make necessary adjustments.

2. Strategies for Data Utilization

Here are key strategies to effectively utilize data for business decisions in your dropshipping venture:

a. Data Collection: Implement systems to collect relevant data, including website analytics, sales data, customer feedback, and market research.

b. Data Analysis: Use data analysis tools and techniques to extract meaningful insights from the collected data. This may involve data visualization, statistical analysis, and predictive modeling.

c. Customer Segmentation: Segment your customer base based on common characteristics and behaviors to personalize marketing and product recommendations.

d. A/B Testing: Conduct A/B tests to compare different strategies or product offerings and determine what resonates best with your audience.

e. Inventory Optimization: Employ data-driven inventory management techniques to minimize holding costs and maximize product availability.

f. Pricing Optimization: Analyze pricing data to set competitive prices while maintaining profitability.

g. Marketing Attribution: Attribute sales and conversions to specific marketing channels to understand the impact of each channel on your business.

h. Customer Lifetime Value (CLV): Calculate CLV to assess the long-term value of your customers and guide marketing and retention efforts.

i. Predictive Analytics: Use predictive analytics to anticipate customer behavior, demand fluctuations, and market trends.

j. Feedback Analysis: Analyze customer feedback and reviews to identify areas for improvement in products and customer service.

k. Reporting: Generate regular reports and dashboards that provide a clear overview of your business's performance and highlight areas that require attention.

3. Data Privacy and Security

Ensure that you handle customer data responsibly, comply with data protection regulations, and implement robust cybersecurity measures to safeguard sensitive information.

4. Data-driven Culture

Foster a data-driven culture within your organization by encouraging employees to use data in their decision-making processes and providing training on data analysis tools and techniques.

5. Continuous Learning

Stay updated on advancements in data analytics and tools to harness the full potential of data for your dropshipping business.

Data-driven decision making is a powerful asset that can drive the success and growth of your dropshipping venture. By collecting, analyzing, and leveraging data effectively, you can make informed decisions that optimize your operations, enhance customer experiences, and stay ahead of the competition. In the following sections, we'll explore additional strategies and best practices for leveraging data and optimizing various aspects of your dropshipping business.

8.2 Exploring Multi-channel Selling

In the ever-evolving world of e-commerce, diversifying your sales channels is a strategic move that can broaden your reach and increase revenue opportunities. Multi-channel selling involves expanding beyond your primary e-commerce platform to reach customers on various online marketplaces and platforms. In this section, we will explore the significance of multi-channel selling and provide strategies for expanding your presence across multiple sales channels.

1. The Power of Multi-channel Selling

Multi-channel selling holds several advantages that can benefit your dropshipping business:

a. Increased Visibility: Expanding to multiple sales channels exposes your products to a broader audience, increasing brand visibility and attracting new customers.

b. Risk Mitigation: Relying on a single platform can be risky. Diversifying your channels reduces dependence on a single source of revenue.

c. Market Reach: Different sales channels may cater to distinct customer demographics, allowing you to tap into new markets and niches.

d. Competitive Edge: Offering your products on various platforms can set you apart from competitors who limit their presence to one channel.

e. Seasonal Opportunities: Multi-channel selling enables you to take advantage of seasonal sales spikes and events on different platforms.

2. Strategies for Multi-channel Selling

Here are key strategies to effectively explore and implement multi-channel selling for your dropshipping business:

a. Platform Selection: Research and select additional sales channels that align with your target audience and product offerings. Common options include Amazon, eBay, Shopify, Etsy, and social media marketplaces.

b. Product Listings: Create optimized product listings tailored to each platform's requirements, including titles, descriptions, and images.

c. Inventory Management: Implement inventory synchronization tools or software to ensure accurate stock levels across all channels and prevent overselling.

d. Pricing Strategy: Develop a pricing strategy that accounts for platform fees, shipping costs, and competitive pricing on each channel.

e. Shipping and Fulfillment: Offer efficient shipping and fulfillment options that meet the expectations of customers on each platform.

f. Brand Consistency: Maintain a consistent brand image and messaging across all channels to build trust and recognition.

g. Customer Support: Provide responsive customer support on each platform to address inquiries and concerns promptly.

h. Marketing Strategies: Tailor your marketing efforts to each channel's audience and promotional features, such as Amazon PPC ads or Instagram Shopping.

i. Analytics and Tracking: Utilize analytics tools to monitor the performance of each channel, measure ROI, and adjust your strategies accordingly.

j. Scaling Gradually: When expanding to new channels, start with a few and gradually add more as you gain experience and resources.

k. Cross-Promotion: Promote your multi-channel presence on your primary e-commerce platform and social media to encourage customers to explore other options.

3. Data Integration

Consider using software or tools that allow for centralized data management and synchronization across multiple sales channels to streamline operations.

4. Platform-Specific Requirements

Familiarize yourself with the unique requirements and policies of each sales channel to ensure compliance and maximize visibility.

5. Inventory Forecasting

Implement data-driven inventory forecasting to optimize stock levels across various sales channels and prevent stockouts or overstocking.

Multi-channel selling can significantly enhance your dropshipping business's reach and revenue potential. By strategically selecting and managing additional sales channels, optimizing your listings and operations, and tailoring your marketing efforts, you can effectively tap into diverse markets and grow your business. In the following sections, we'll explore additional strategies and best practices for expanding and optimizing various aspects of your dropshipping venture.

8.3 Customization and Private Labeling

Customization and private labeling are powerful strategies to differentiate your dropshipping business and establish a unique brand identity. These approaches allow you to offer personalized products or sell under your own brand name, giving you a competitive edge in the market. In this section, we will explore the significance of customization and private labeling and provide strategies for their effective implementation.

1. The Value of Customization and Private Labeling

Customization and private labeling offer several advantages for your dropshipping business:

a. Brand Identity: Private labeling allows you to create a distinct brand identity and establish brand recognition among customers.

b. Product Uniqueness: Customization enables you to offer unique products tailored to your target audience's preferences and needs.

c. Competitive Differentiation: In a crowded marketplace, customization and private labeling set you apart from competitors selling generic products.

d. Customer Loyalty: Personalized products and branded offerings can foster customer loyalty and repeat business.

e. Higher Profit Margins: Private labeling often allows for higher profit margins as customers perceive added value in branded products.

2. Customization Strategies

Implementing customization in your dropshipping business involves the following strategies:

a. Product Personalization: Offer products that customers can customize with their names, images, or messages, such as personalized jewelry, apparel, or home decor.

b. Variations and Options: Provide product variations, colors, sizes, and features that customers can choose to tailor products to their preferences.

c. Design Your Own: Allow customers to design their own products through interactive design tools on your website.

d. Bundling and Kits: Create customized product bundles or kits that cater to specific needs or themes.

e. Made-to-Order: Offer made-to-order products where customers can select the materials, colors, and specifications of their products.

3. Private Labeling Strategies

To implement private labeling effectively, consider the following strategies:

a. Supplier Partnerships: Establish partnerships with suppliers or manufacturers who offer private labeling services.

b. Brand Development: Create a compelling brand identity, including a brand name, logo, and packaging design.

c. Product Selection: Choose products that align with your brand and target audience, and work with suppliers to apply your branding.

d. Quality Control: Ensure that private-labeled products meet your quality standards and specifications.

e. Inventory Management: Manage your private-labeled product inventory effectively to avoid overstocking or stockouts.

f. Pricing Strategy: Price your private-labeled products competitively while maintaining profitability.

g. Marketing and Promotion: Promote your private-labeled products through your marketing channels to build brand awareness.

4. Branding Consistency

Maintain consistency in branding across all your private-labeled products to reinforce your brand identity and credibility.

5. Market Research

Conduct market research to identify opportunities for customization and private labeling that align with market trends and customer preferences.

6. Supplier Relationships

Build strong relationships with suppliers or manufacturers who can provide customization or private labeling services and meet your quality standards.

Customization and private labeling offer unique opportunities to create a distinctive brand and cater to customer preferences. By implementing these strategies effectively, you can differentiate your dropshipping business in a competitive market, foster customer loyalty, and potentially increase profit margins. In the following sections, we'll explore additional strategies and best practices for enhancing various aspects of your dropshipping venture.

8.4 Building a Sustainable Business Model

Sustainability is a key consideration in today's business landscape, and it goes beyond environmental responsibility. In the context of your dropshipping venture, a sustainable business model encompasses practices that not only promote long-term growth and profitability but also ensure ethical and responsible business operations. In this section, we will explore the significance of building a sustainable business model and provide strategies for its effective implementation.

1. The Essence of a Sustainable Business Model

A sustainable business model is designed to endure and thrive over the long term by addressing various dimensions of sustainability:

a. Financial Sustainability: The ability to maintain profitability, manage expenses, and generate consistent revenue to support ongoing operations and growth.

b. Environmental Responsibility: Minimizing the environmental impact of your business by adopting eco-friendly practices and reducing waste.

c. Social Responsibility: Ensuring ethical and fair treatment of employees, suppliers, and customers while contributing positively to the community.

d. Customer-Centricity: Prioritizing customer satisfaction, loyalty, and trust by delivering quality products and exceptional service.

e. Adaptability: The capability to adapt to market changes, emerging trends, and customer preferences while remaining competitive.

2. Strategies for Building a Sustainable Business Model

Here are key strategies to build a sustainable business model for your dropshipping venture:

a. Ethical Sourcing: Partner with suppliers who adhere to ethical and sustainable practices, such as fair labor conditions and responsible sourcing of materials.

b. Quality Assurance: Ensure the quality and safety of the products you sell to build trust with customers and reduce returns and disputes.

c. Transparency: Be transparent about your business practices, product origins, and environmental efforts, fostering trust and loyalty among customers.

d. Minimal Environmental Impact: Implement eco-friendly packaging, energy-efficient operations, and responsible waste management practices.

e. Responsible Pricing: Offer competitive prices that reflect fair value for customers and sustainable profitability for your business.

f. Social Engagement: Engage with your community or support social causes aligned with your brand values to demonstrate social responsibility.

g. Continuous Improvement: Continuously assess and improve your business practices, product offerings, and customer experiences.

h. Employee Well-being: Prioritize the well-being and professional development of your employees, fostering a positive and productive work environment.

i. Long-term Vision: Develop a long-term vision and strategic plan that aligns with sustainable growth and ethical principles.

j. Customer Feedback: Collect and analyze customer feedback to make improvements and meet evolving customer expectations.

k. Compliance and Regulations: Stay informed about industry regulations and compliance standards related to e-commerce and dropshipping.

l. Risk Management: Identify and mitigate risks that could impact your business's sustainability, such as supply chain disruptions or market fluctuations.

m. Innovation: Explore innovative solutions and technologies that can enhance your business's sustainability efforts and operational efficiency.

3. Measurement and Reporting

Establish key performance indicators (KPIs) and metrics to measure your business's sustainability efforts and regularly report progress to stakeholders.

4. Industry Certification

Consider obtaining industry certifications or endorsements related to sustainability, which can enhance your brand's credibility.

A sustainable business model is not only beneficial for the environment and society but also essential for long-term success and competitiveness. By incorporating ethical and responsible practices into your dropshipping operations and continuously improving your sustainability efforts, you can build a business that thrives while contributing positively to the world. In the following sections, we'll explore additional strategies and best practices to optimize various aspects of your dropshipping venture.

Conclusion: Summary of Key Takeaways

Congratulations on completing "Maximizing Profits with WooCommerce: The Ultimate Guide to Dropshipping from AliExpress." Throughout this comprehensive guide, we've covered every aspect of building, growing, and scaling a successful dropshipping business. As you reflect on your journey, let's summarize the key takeaways that will help you succeed in the world of dropshipping:

1. Understanding Dropshipping: The Basics:
   - Dropshipping is a business model that allows you to sell products without holding inventory.
   - AliExpress is a popular platform for finding dropshipping suppliers and products.

2. Why Choose WooCommerce and AliExpress?:
   - WooCommerce is a powerful e-commerce platform that seamlessly integrates with WordPress.
   - AliExpress offers a vast catalog of products, competitive prices, and reliable shipping options for dropshippers.

3. Setting Up Your Online Store:
   - Choose a domain name and hosting that align with your brand and business.
   - Install and configure WooCommerce to transform your WordPress website into an online store.

4. Essential WooCommerce Settings for Dropshipping:
   - Configure settings related to taxes, shipping, payments, and product management.
   - Ensure your store's security with an SSL certificate.

5. Designing a User-Friendly Website:
   - Select a responsive theme for your store.
   - Optimize page loading speed and ensure intuitive navigation.
   - Use high-quality product images and compelling product descriptions.

6. Integrating AliExpress with WooCommerce:
   - Find reliable AliExpress suppliers with a strong track record.
   - Import products to your store and set competitive pricing.

7. Enhancing Your Store with Essential Plugins:
   - Explore essential plugins to streamline your operations, improve product listings, and enhance customer experience.
   - Automate order processing and inventory management.

8. Mastering Dropshipping Operations:
   - Manage supplier relationships effectively.
   - Automate order fulfillment, track inventory, and provide excellent customer service.
   - Scale your business while maintaining efficiency.

9. Marketing Your Dropshipping Store:
   - Develop a comprehensive marketing plan.
   - Utilize content marketing, SEO, social media, email marketing, and paid advertising to reach your audience.
   - Monitor and analyze marketing efforts to refine your strategies.

10. Scaling Your Dropshipping Business:
    - Expand your product catalog and explore new markets.
    - Optimize inventory management and order fulfillment.
    - Focus on customer retention and loyalty.

11. Legal and Financial Considerations:
    - Choose the right business structure and ensure legal compliance.
    - Protect intellectual property and handle data privacy.
    - Manage taxes, insurance, and financial matters prudently.

12. Advanced Dropshipping Strategies:
    - Source from multiple suppliers and consider private labeling.
    - Expand internationally and explore subscription models.
    - Implement cross-selling, upselling, and marketplace diversification.
    - Foster customer loyalty through advanced marketing tactics.

As you embark on your dropshipping journey or refine your existing business, remember that success in this field requires continuous learning and adaptation. Stay updated with industry trends, engage with your audience, and keep refining your strategies.

Thank you for choosing this guide as your resource for dropshipping success. We wish you all the best in your dropshipping endeavors, and may your business thrive and prosper in the ever-evolving world of e-commerce. Happy dropshipping!

Future Trends in Dropshipping

As the e-commerce landscape continues to evolve, dropshipping is also poised to undergo significant changes and advancements. Staying ahead of the curve and embracing emerging trends can give your dropshipping business a competitive edge. Here are some future trends in dropshipping to keep an eye on:

1. Sustainable and Eco-Friendly Products:

Consumers are increasingly conscious of the environmental impact of their purchases. As a result, there's a growing demand for sustainable and eco-friendly products. Consider adding such products to your dropshipping inventory to cater to this environmentally conscious audience.

2. Local and Domestic Sourcing:

With a focus on faster shipping and reduced carbon footprint, dropshippers may increasingly turn to local and domestic suppliers. This trend could lead to shorter delivery times, improved quality control, and support for local businesses.

3. Micro-Moments and Mobile Shopping:

Micro-moments, where consumers make quick purchasing decisions on their mobile devices, are on the rise. Ensure that your dropshipping store is mobile-friendly and optimized for seamless mobile shopping experiences.

4. AI and Automation:

Artificial intelligence (AI) and automation technologies will continue to play a significant role in dropshipping. AI can assist with customer support, data analysis, and even product recommendations, enhancing the overall shopping experience.

5. Personalization:

Consumers appreciate personalized experiences. Utilize data-driven insights to personalize product recommendations, email marketing, and user interfaces, creating a tailored shopping journey for each customer.

6. Augmented Reality (AR) and Virtual Reality (VR):

AR and VR technologies are becoming more accessible. Implementing these technologies can enable customers to visualize products in their environment before making a purchase, reducing buyer uncertainty.

7. Multi-Channel Selling:

Expanding beyond your WooCommerce store to sell on various e-commerce platforms and marketplaces (e.g., Amazon, eBay, Shopify) can help you reach a broader audience and diversify your sales channels.

8. Cryptocurrency Payments:

The adoption of cryptocurrencies as a form of payment is increasing. Consider integrating cryptocurrency payment options into your online store to cater to tech-savvy customers.

9. Niche Markets and Micro-Niches:

Identifying and targeting specific niche markets or even micro-niches can be a successful strategy. By offering highly specialized products, you can become a go-to source for a dedicated customer base.

10. Sustainability in Packaging and Shipping:

Eco-friendly packaging and sustainable shipping practices will become more critical. Consider using recyclable or biodegradable packaging materials and offering carbon-neutral shipping options.

11. Voice Commerce:

With the proliferation of voice-activated devices like Amazon Echo and Google Home, voice commerce is on the rise. Ensure your products are optimized for voice search and voice-activated shopping.

12. Customer Experience Enhancement:

Investing in exceptional customer experiences, from personalized interactions to hassle-free returns, will remain a priority. Happy customers are more likely to become repeat buyers and brand advocates.

By staying informed about these future trends in dropshipping and adapting your business strategies accordingly, you can position your dropshipping venture for long-term success in an ever-evolving e-commerce landscape. Embrace innovation, keep an eye on consumer preferences, and remain flexible in your approach to thrive in this dynamic industry.

WooCommerce Plugins:

1. WooCommerce: The core plugin for building and managing your online store.

2. WooCommerce Subscriptions: If you plan to offer subscription-based products or services, this extension makes it easy to set up and manage recurring payments.

3. WooCommerce Bookings: Ideal for businesses offering appointment-based services or rental products, this plugin allows customers to book appointments or rentals directly from your website.

4. WooCommerce Memberships: If you want to create a membership-based website with restricted access to content or products, this plugin helps manage memberships and access control.

5. WooCommerce Product Add-Ons: Allows you to offer customizations and additional options for your products, such as personalized engraving or gift wrapping.

6. WooCommerce PDF Invoices & Packing Slips: Generate professional invoices and packing slips for

your customers' orders.

7. WooCommerce Social Login: Simplify the registration and login process for customers by allowing them to log in using their social media accounts.

8. WooCommerce Subscriptions: If you plan to offer subscription-based products or services, this extension makes it easy to set up and manage recurring payments.

AliExpress Plugins:

1. AliDropship: A comprehensive AliExpress dropshipping plugin that simplifies product import, order processing, and inventory management.

2. Ali2Woo: This plugin allows you to import AliExpress products directly into your WooCommerce store, complete with product details and images.

3. Dropified: While not specific to AliExpress, Dropified is a powerful dropshipping platform that supports AliExpress integration along with other suppliers.

4. Oberlo: Although primarily designed for Shopify, Oberlo is a popular option for dropshipping from AliExpress, allowing for product import and order automation.

5. WooCommerce AliExpress Dropshipping: A WooCommerce-specific plugin for importing AliExpress products, managing pricing, and fulfilling orders.

6. CJDropshipping: CJDropshipping offers a WooCommerce integration plugin to connect your store with their platform, which provides access to a wide range of suppliers.

7. WooCommerce Dropshipping by CedCommerce: This plugin streamlines the dropshipping process, allowing you to import products from AliExpress and automate order fulfillment.

8. Alibaba Importer: If you're also interested in sourcing products from Alibaba, this plugin helps you import and manage products from this platform.

Remember to research and carefully evaluate each plugin based on your specific business needs, as their features and compatibility may vary. Additionally, check for customer reviews, support, and updates to ensure you're using reliable and up-to-date solutions for your WooCommerce and AliExpress dropshipping store.

1. WooCommerce Documentation: The official WooCommerce documentation is a valuable resource for learning how to use the platform effectively. It includes detailed guides, tutorials, and troubleshooting tips: [WooCommerce Documentation](https://docs.woocommerce.com/).

2. AliExpress Dropshipping Center: AliExpress provides a dedicated dropshipping center with resources, guides, and tools to assist dropshippers. You can find product research, marketing tips, and more: [AliExpress Dropshipping Center](https://sale.aliexpress.com/ru/__pc/dropshipping_learn_more.htm).

3. WooCommerce Community: Join the WooCommerce Community forums to connect with other

users, ask questions, and share experiences. It's a great place to seek advice and solutions to common issues: [WooCommerce Community](https://woocommerce.com/community/).

4. WordPress.org Support: If you encounter issues with your WordPress website, the official WordPress support forums are a valuable resource for troubleshooting and getting assistance: [WordPress.org Support Forums](https://wordpress.org/support/).

5. Online Courses and Tutorials: Consider enrolling in online courses or watching video tutorials on platforms like Udemy, Coursera, or YouTube. Many experts share their insights on WooCommerce and dropshipping strategies.

6. E-commerce Blogs and Forums: Keep up with industry trends and gain insights from e-commerce blogs and forums like Shopify's eCommerce University, BigCommerce Community, or Reddit's /r/ecommerce.

7. Books and E-books: Explore e-commerce and dropshipping books that provide in-depth knowledge and strategies for success. Check out platforms like Amazon or your local bookstore for relevant titles.

8. Social Media and LinkedIn Groups: Join e-commerce and dropshipping groups on social media platforms like Facebook, LinkedIn, and Reddit to connect with fellow entrepreneurs and share experiences.

9. Dropshipping Tools and Software Providers: Many dropshipping tool providers offer educational resources, webinars, and support to help you use their tools effectively. Check with the tools you're using for such resources.

10. E-commerce Conferences and Webinars: Attend industry conferences, webinars, and workshops to stay updated on the latest e-commerce trends and network with other professionals.

11. Mentorship and Coaching: Consider seeking mentorship or coaching from experienced e-commerce and dropshipping entrepreneurs who can provide personalized guidance and insights.

12. Podcasts: Listen to e-commerce and dropshipping podcasts where experts share their experiences, tips, and strategies. Some popular options include "My Wife Quit Her Job," "The EcomCrew Podcast," and "The Dropshipping Secrets Podcast."

Remember that the e-commerce and dropshipping landscapes are constantly evolving, so staying informed and continuously learning is essential for long-term success. Tailor your learning journey to your specific needs and goals, and don't hesitate to seek support and advice from the vast community of e-commerce entrepreneurs and experts.

www.ingramcontent.com/pod-product-compliance
Lightning Source LLC
Chambersburg PA
CBHW082217220526
45470CB00010B/3211